Open Strategy for Digital Business

This book offers the reader a novel perspective on how digital contexts and open strategy approaches – the act of opening up strategic initiatives beyond company managers to involve front-line employees, stakeholders, and entrepreneurs – are related.

Going beyond the claim that digital media drives open strategy by containing a detailed analyses of the interrelations between the two, the authors examine how ICT have diffused globally and trace the emerging links between digitally driven environments and open strategizing approaches. This book also draws a general picture of how and why digital technologies create new networks. A more competitive, transparent, empowered, and inclusive environment would enhance development and encourage novel approaches to strategies implemented. Real-life exemplifications of how and why digital technologies contribute to open strategizing are also provided. Various drivers impacting the necessity to develop more relational advantage are discussed and intertwined with the description of challenges observed in the case of imposing openness.

A useful resource for researchers of strategic management and information systems, as well as those looking at digital strategy and transformation.

Ewa Lechman is Professor of Economics, employed at Faculty of Management and Economics, Gdańsk University of Technology/Fahrenheit Universities. Her research interests are digital technology, innovations, economic development, social development, and financial innovations.

Joanna Radomska is Associate Professor in the Strategic Management Department and Vice-Dean of the Faculty of Business and Management at Wrocław University of Economics and Business. Her research interest falls under management, including open strategy, omnichannel, strategy practice, creative industries, and family business areas.

Ewa Stańczyk-Hugiet is Professor in the Advanced Research in Management Department at Wroclaw University of Economics. Her research interest falls under the broad scope of management studies, including open strategizing, strategic management and elements of organizational adaptation, and inter-organizational dynamics in complex environment.

Routledge Focus on Business and Management

The fields of business and management have grown exponentially as areas of research and education. This growth presents challenges for readers trying to keep up with the latest important insights. *Routledge Focus on Business and Management* presents small books on big topics and how they intersect with the world of business research.

Individually, each title in the series provides coverage of a key academic topic, whilst collectively, the series forms a comprehensive collection across the business disciplines.

Entrepreneurial Attributes
Accessing Your Inner Entrepreneur For Business and Beyond
Andrew Clarke

Leadership and Strategic Management
Decision-Making in Times of Change
Paolo Boccardelli and Federica Brunetta

Artificial Intelligence and Project Management
An Integrated Approach to Knowledge-Based Evaluation
Tadeusz A. Grzeszczyk

Organizational Aesthetics
Artful Visual Representations of Business and Organizations
Barbara Fryzel and Aleksander Marcinkowski

Open Strategy for Digital Business
Managing in ICT-Driven Environments
Ewa Lechman, Joanna Radomska, and Ewa Stańczyk-Hugiet

For more information about this series, please visit: www.routledge.com/Routledge-Focus-on-Business-and-Management/book-series/FBM

Open Strategy for Digital Business

Managing in ICT-Driven Environments

Ewa Lechman, Joanna Radomska, and Ewa Stańczyk-Hugiet

Routledge
Taylor & Francis Group

LONDON AND NEW YORK

First published 2024
by Routledge
4 Park Square, Milton Park, Abingdon, Oxon, OX14 4RN

and by Routledge
605 Third Avenue, New York, NY 10158

Routledge is an imprint of the Taylor & Francis Group, an informa business

© 2024 Ewa Lechman, Joanna Radomska, and Ewa Stańczyk-Hugiet

The right of Ewa Lechman, Joanna Radomska, and Ewa Stańczyk-Hugiet to be identified as author of this work has been asserted in accordance with sections 77 and 78 of the Copyright, Designs and Patents Act 1988.

Trademark notice: Product or corporate names may be trademarks or registered trademarks, and are used only for identification and explanation without intent to infringe.

British Library Cataloguing-in-Publication Data
A catalogue record for this book is available from the British Library

Library of Congress Cataloging-in-Publication Data
Names: Lechman, Ewa, author. | Radomska, Joanna, author. | Stańczyk-Hugiet, Ewa, author.
Title: Open strategy for digital business : managing in ICT-driven environments / Ewa Lechman, Joanna Radomska, and Ewa Stańczyk-Hugiet.
Description: Abingdon, Oxon ; New York, NY : Routledge, 2025. | Series: Routledge focus on business and management | Includes bibliographical references and index.
Identifiers: LCCN 2024014938 (print) | LCCN 2024014939 (ebook) | ISBN 9781032544175 (hardback) | ISBN 9781032544182 (paperback) | ISBN 9781003424772 (ebook)
Subjects: LCSH: Industrial management—Technological innovations. | Management information systems.
Classification: LCC HD30.213 .L43 2025 (print) | LCC HD30.213 (ebook) | DDC 658.4/038—dc23/eng/20240410
LC record available at https://lccn.loc.gov/2024014938
LC ebook record available at https://lccn.loc.gov/2024014939

ISBN: 978-1-032-54417-5 (hbk)
ISBN: 978-1-032-54418-2 (pbk)
ISBN: 978-1-003-42477-2 (ebk)

DOI: 10.4324/9781003424772

Typeset in Times New Roman
by Apex CoVantage, LLC

Contents

More about the authors

Ewa Lechman is a professor of economics, employed at Faculty of Management and Economics, Gdańsk University of Technology/Fahrenheit Universities. Her research interests concentrate on economic development, digital technologies and technological progress, and its role in reshaping social and economic systems, as well as economics of network and innovative financial instruments. Serves as permanent referee in more than 35 highly ranked academic journals. In 2013 she was an Emerald Literati Network Award for Excellence winner; in 2017–2019 she was nominated by Elsevier as outstanding reviewer. In several years her academic track records contributed to University's *Elsevier Research Impact Leaders Award*. Co-ordinated and participated in multiple research grants on digital technologies, social and economic development awarded by, *inter alia*, National Science Centre, CERGE-Global Development Network, National Bank of Poland, Stockholm Business School, United Nations for Development Program, EU-funds. An author and co-author of more than 120 papers and books. Serves as editor in Telecommunication Policy journal (Elsevier). A former vice-dean for development and PhD program director. Co-operated with ECSB, CEEMAN, BMDA, AMBA, and Eurostat. Servers in advisory board of Gdansk Business Club.

Joanna Radomska is an associate professor in the Strategic Management Department and vice-dean of the Faculty of Business and Management at Wrocław University of Economics and Business. Her research interests cover the fields of open strategy, omnichannel, strategy-as-practice, strategy implementation, creative industries, and family business. She authored and co-authored 80 book chapters and articles. She is a reviewer at several journals (i.e., *International Business Review*, *Benchmarking*, *Journal of Organizational Change Management*) and conferences (EMAC, EURAM, EIBA). She has been engaged in several research projects in strategic management, strategy implementation, employee engagement, and change management. She has been awarded two research grants from the National Science Centre in Poland. She is working on the Horizon project (Games, Heritage, Arts, & Sport: Exploring the Economic, Social, and Cultural Value of the European Video Game Industry Ecosystem) in collaboration with universities and organizations (i.e., City Football Group and Ubisoft).

Ewa Stańczyk-Hugiet is a professor in the Advanced Research in Management Department at Wroclaw University of Economics. Her research circulates around the field of strategic management, knowledge management, and inter-organizational networks. Her evolutionary view of strategic management contributes to a deeper understanding of organizational adaptation and inter-organizational dynamics in complex environment. She is a recognized reviewer in doctoral and professorship procedures, in research projects grants, as well as articles for renowned journals, as evidenced by the Emerald Literati Award for Excellence in the Outstanding Reviewer category (2022). She participated in numerous research projects. Previously, she served as a dean of the faculty (2016–2019). Since 2021 she has served as vice-rector for research and academic staff. She has been involved in the Committee on Organisation and Management Sciences of the Polish Academy of Sciences. She was awarded the title of doctor honoris causa (2023) for scientific and organizational achievements.

1 Introduction

1.1 Setting the context

Doing business is not digitally neutral. Technological progress as a disruptive process alters social and economic structures, stimulating the emergence of a new *status quo*. Technology not only brings change or inventions to the economy and society; it enriches and shapes socioeconomic systems, enhancing their responsiveness and adaptability to further technological change. The latter demonstrates the interrelatedness of society, economy, and technology, driving home that none of these elements exist in isolation.

Digital technologies (ICT) are widely acknowledged as the critical drivers for knowledge and information acquisition, labour and capital productivity, and social, political, and economic empowerment (Graham, 2019). Due to the strong externalities (Katz & Shapiro, 1985), these technologies enable the emergence of various networks reshaping the way that businesses are run, trading and consumption patterns, economic and social behaviours, social norms and attitudes (Graham & Dutton, 2019).

Empirical research tracing societies' and economies' sensitivity to the introduction of digital technologies discusses a variety of channels of impact between and interrelations between these two. Earlier studies concentrated predominantly on creating network societies and economies (Shapiro & Varian, 1988; Castells, 2000 and 2011; Johansson et al., 2012; Van Dijk, 2020), information societies (Mossberger et al., 2007; Beniger, 2009; Lyon, 2013; Buckland, 2017; Martin, 2017) where structural changes are driven by solid network externalities (Katz & Shapiro, 1985) and unlimited access to all types of information and knowledge usually at negligible marginal cost. Other studies emphasized the purely technical side of technological progress that changes the production structure and consumption side (Joyce et al., 2019). The effects of technological progress on the economy's supply and demand side are relatively direct and immediate. At the same time, changes in ways of making business and trading patterns (Rodríguez-Crespo & Martínez-Zarzoso, 2019), education and skills (Livingstone, 2012), labour markets and labour force (Falk & Biagi, 2017),

DOI: 10.4324/9781003424772-1

people's economic engagement, or – more broadly – productivity shifts seem to be more hidden, indirect, and unveiled in a long-term perspective. Theoretical and empirical academic contributions highlight different positive effects that digital technologies may generate, contributing to the general welfare of individuals, companies, businesses, and whole societies by offering them new opportunities in education and skills improvements, setting up a new business, or improving those already existing and arising from gradually increasing the use of ICT worldwide. Starting from contributing works of, for example, Abramovitz (1986), Dosi et al. (1988), Freeman and Soete (1990), Fagerberg (1994 and 1995), Fagerberg et al. (1994) to more recent evidence like, for instance, works of Bilan et al. (2019), Loh and Chib (2019), Tchamyou et al. (2019), Adam (2020), Ali et al. (2020), or Vu et al. (2020) massive literature documents both conceptual frameworks and empirical evidence regarding ICT impact on social and economic development. Also, we found relevant literature linking economic geography and brand management, which supports the fact that intangibles being – to a significant extent – the 'effect' of digital innovations and solutions, such as brands, can strongly influence economic growth (Pike, 2009, 2015; Kucharska et al., 2018). Moreover, for economies like, for example, the US, South Korea, and Japan, electronics and software engendering images of their countries are causally linked with the pictures of critical sectors existing in these countries (Ferilli et al., 2016).

Digital technologies pave avenues to bring businesses to operate in a more inclusive and more transparent environment. However, digital technologies such as General Purpose Technologies empower various collaborative network creation and expansion, reshaping the business and formulating strategies. As the newly emerged digitally driven environment pushes companies to adjust to stay competitive and grow in global markets, there is also an urgent need to reshape 'classical' business strategies to novel ones where much emphasis will be put on effective operationalization in the global, digital economy. The concept of open strategizing, where transparency, empowerment, and inclusiveness play fundamental roles, seems to suit ideally.

The capability to adapt to environmental context demands, which results in growing challenges regarding the strategy selection problem, is highly crucial (e.g. Marewski et al., 2018). Organizational adaptability is the ability to react swiftly to new business opportunities, adapt to highly changeable market environments, and drive the organization's transformation (Birkinshaw & Gibson, 2004). Among these drivers, we may mention the growing technological advancements, hyper-dynamics of markets, and various digitalization pressures that bring the growing need to build inter-organizational relationships (Klimas et al., 2021). Another group of drivers that covers societal pressures and the changing flexibility of organizational boundaries also gives the ground for opening different strategic areas (Whittington, 2019). Finally, the unexpected shifts brought by the appearance of wild cards, such as pandemics, also challenged the already-established praxes and developed more collaborative responses (Chesbrough, 2020).

Indeed, a more open strategy approach may facilitate the required strategic flexibility (Jarzabkowski, 2004). Open strategy is defined as a 'dynamic bundle of practices that affords internal and external actors greater strategic transparency and/or inclusion' (Hautz et al., 2017, pp. 298–299). Therefore, flexibility is driven by four factors: transparency, inclusion, participation, and IT-enablement (Whittington et al., 2011; Seidl et al., 2019). To explore the practices, the strategizing routines are discussed as they link different everyday strategy practices through their identities and specific experiences. Organizational routines' role in strategizing highlights the importance of constructing and replicating strategy practices. This work explores how strategy practices, that is, routines, affect strategizing and contributes to strategy research by explicating the influence of organizational routines on more open strategizing practices. Indeed, the research problem revolves around how practices might be utilized over time as open organizing remains undertheorized (Lingo, 2023).

Further, scholars, with few exceptions (Luedicke et al., 2017), have tended to examine open strategy efforts focused on either internal or external perspectives rather than multiple, different types of stakeholders, such as employees, customers, and vendors, simultaneously (Von Krogh & Geilenger, 2019). That is the path we want to follow, trying to grasp the multidimensional perspective and provide a conceptual framework linking open strategy dimensions with the recognized patterns used to understand how open strategic activity is undertaken. Hence, due to their collective character, there is a direct connection between organizational routines and practices. Therefore, we apply the processual lenses to investigate open strategizing on different organizational levels. Finally, we outline the impact of ICT and digital economies that create an environment where open strategizing brings more benefits than standard practices, as innovativeness, transparency, empowerment, and inclusion are essential to respond to emerging challenges.

1.2 What does this book offer?

This book offers a novel perspective linking digital technologies with open strategizing approaches. It is designed to provide deep insight into elements exploring open strategizing in the context of digital technology. It identifies the nature of the digital economy and how and through which channel the digital environment's impact affects and profoundly reshapes current approaches to designing strategies. It draws a general picture of how and why digital technologies, by creating new networks and a more competitive, transparent, empowered, and inclusive environment, enhance development and adopt novel approaches to strategies implemented. Various drivers impacting the necessity to develop more relational advantage are discussed and intertwined with the description of challenges observed in the case of imposing openness. Finally, the internal aspect of organizational routines is also investigated, allowing us to explore the multidimensional analysis framework. More specifically, our significant contribution consists of

- identifying the nature of digital technologies and how they enable an open strategizing approach to manage companies in an ICT-driven environment;
- tracing the potentially emerging links between a digitally driven environment and open strategizing approaches;
- exploring the routines in the strategizing process by extending the scope of strategic studies and going beyond top managers to gain deeper insights; and
- investigating open strategizing by applying the processual lenses.

1.3   Book structure

This book comprises five chapters. The first chapter is the Introduction itself. It sets the broad background and general context of the book. It comprehensively justifies how and why digital technologies and an ICT-driven economy create a favourable environment for a novel approach to companies' management: open strategizing. It also contextualizes the open strategizing concept, emphasizing its significant advantages compared to 'traditional approaches', explaining how and why it allows companies to head towards higher effectiveness and gain a more stable market position. The introductory chapter also discusses the book's significant aims and scopes and presents the content of the remaining chapters.

Chapter 2, 'Open strategizing', provides a comprehensive view of open strategizing with its restrictions, triggers, and enablers. It briefly discusses the idea of 'openness' using processual lenses to outline the shift toward greater transparency and inclusion in the strategizing processes directed by leveraging different forms of openness and closure. It focuses on open strategizing and discusses the previous streams of research, emphasizing considered limitations and identifying further directions.

Next, Chapter 3, 'Digital technologies. The paving road ahead towards open strategizing?', provides the reader with a more specific conceptual and theoretical background regarding the ideas behind the techno-economic paradigms (regimes). It broadly presents the concept of 'techno-economic regimes'. It emphasizes that the in-time behaviour of the evolutionary system, combining society and technologies, is driven by societies' culture, preferences, attitudes, and risk aversion, which drive individual decisions in whether to accept or reject newly emerging technological solutions. It also discusses the ongoing 'digital revolution' as the Fifth Technological Revolution. It stresses the unique features of digital technologies and how they can contribute to open strategizing – however, these links shall be explored more deeply in the following chapters. This part also traces the unique characteristics of digital technologies and the values they bring to the digitally driven business environment. Finally, to draw the general context of the remainder of the book, it provides a global overview of ICT development in recent decades.

Chapter 4, 'Strategic Practices in the Digital Context. Tracing challenges', discusses the strategy process exploiting mainly the strategy-as-practice approach as one of the central theoretical debates in the strategy area. It shows how digital technology is changing the nature of strategizing, showing that open strategy is an emerging information technology (IT)-enabled strategizing practice. This chapter discusses different organizational, managerial, and individual aspects influencing strategizing in a digital context. Furthermore, it claims that strategizing practices are usually routinized, linking different entities constructing everyday strategy practices through their identities and specific experiences as strategy practitioners. Organizational practices' role in strategizing highlights the importance of structuring and replicating strategy practices. The capability perspective, especially the dynamic capabilities framework explaining how firms respond to rapid technology, is also essential to discuss from an IT-enabled practices perspective. Lastly, specifying selected organizational, managerial, and individual aspects regarding strategic organizational practices that have evolved under the influence of ICT, this part shows how these drivers affect strategizing practices by explaining their impact on open strategizing with digital enablement.

Chapter 5 deals with 'Digital technologies as drivers of strategizing practices'. Based on the insights, it explores the factors that may foster or hinder the open strategizing process, focusing on essential digital drivers in this context. The focus of the presentation will be the nexus between information systems and open strategy practice and the impact of digitalization on the format of the open strategy process. It presents digital work tools used in strategizing practices, leading to reconfiguring work practices toward open strategizing. Moreover, a synthesis of good and bad practices will be presented using specific real-life exemplifications to present and evaluate how IT and open strategizing practices can act as a platform for organizational transformation. Specifically, the exemplifications will address inclusiveness, openness, and transparency. Lastly, we discuss the consequences of using digital technologies in strategy practice. Furthermore, a discussion on how to create and use a digital environment for openness, innovativeness, empowerment, and inclusion as essential to be effective in a digitally shaped context will be provided.

Finally, Chapter 6, 'Concluding remarks', provides the summary of our findings, emphasizing the most fundamental implications and further research direction.

References

Abramovitz, M. (1986). Catching up, forging ahead, and falling behind. *Journal of Economic History*, 385–406.

Adam, D. (2020). Special report: The simulations driving the world's response to COVID-19. *Nature, 580*(7802), 316–319.

Ali, M. A., Alam, K., Taylor, B., & Rafiq, S. (2020). Does ICT maturity catalyse economic development? Evidence from a panel data estimation approach in OECD countries. *Economic Analysis and Policy.* https://doi. org/10.1016/j.eap.2020.09.003

Ali, O., Shrestha, A., Osmanaj, V., & Muhammed, S. (2020). Cloud computing technology adoption: an evaluation of key factors in local governments. *Information Technology & People, 34*(2), 666–703.

Beniger, J. (2009). *The control revolution: Technological and economic origins of the information society.* Harvard University Press.

Bilan, Y., Rubanov, P., Vasylieva, T., & Lyeonov, S. (2019). The influence of industry 4.0 on financial services: Determinants of alternative finance development. *Polish Journal of management studies, 19*(1), 70–93.

Bilan, Y., Mishchuk, H., Samoliuk, N., & Grishnova, O. (2019). ICT and economic growth: Links and possibilities of engaging. *Intellectual Economics, 13*(1), 93–104.

Birkinshaw, J., & Gibson, C. (2004). Building ambidexterity into an organization. *MIT Sloan Management Review, 45*, 47–55.

Buckland, M. (2017). *Information and society.* MIT Press.

Castells, M. (2000). Toward a sociology of the network society. *Contemporary Sociology, 29*(5), 693–699.

Castells, M. (2011). *The rise of the network society* (Vol. 12). John Wiley & Sons.

Castells, M., & Cardoso, G. (Eds.). (2006). *The network society: From knowledge to policy* (pp. 3–23). Johns Hopkins Center for Transatlantic Relations.

Chesbrough, H. (2020). To recover faster from Covid-19, open up: Managerial implications from an open innovation perspective. *Industrial Marketing Management, 88*, 410–413.

Dosi, G., Freeman, C., Nelson, R., Silverberg, G., & Soete, L. (1988). *Technical change and economic theory.* Laboratory of Economics and Management (LEM), Sant'Anna School of Advanced Studies.

Fagerberg, J. (1994). Technology and international differences in growth rates. *Journal of Economic Literature, 32*(3), 1147–1175.

Fagerberg, J. (1995). Convergence or divergence? The impact of technology on "why growth rates differ". *Journal of Evolutionary Economics, 5*(3), 269–284.

Fagerberg, J., Verspagen, B., & von Tunzelmann, G. N. (1994). *The dynamics of technology, trade and growth.* Edward Elgar Publishing.

Falk, M., & Biagi, F. (2017). Relative demand for highly skilled workers and use of different ICT technologies. *Applied Economics, 49*(9), 903–914.

Ferilli, G., Sacco, P. L., Teti, E., & Buscema, M. (2016). Top corporate brands and the global structure of country brand positioning: An AutoCM ANN approach. *Expert Systems with Applications, 66*, 62–75.

Freeman, C., & Soete, L. (1990). Information technology, and the global economy. In *The information society: Evolving landscapes* (pp. 278–294). Springer.

Graham, M. (Ed.). (2019). *Digital economies at global margins.* MIT Press.

Graham, M., & Dutton, W. H. (Eds.). (2019). *Society and the internet: How networks of information and communication are changing our lives*. Oxford University Press.

Hautz, J., Seidl, D., & Whittington, R. (2017). Open strategy: Dimensions, dilemmas, dynamics. *Long Range Planning*, *50*(3), 298–309.

Jarzabkowski, P. (2004). Strategy as practice: Recursiveness, adaptation, and practices-in-use. *Organization Studies*, *25*(4), 529–560.

Johansson, B., Karlsson, C., & Westin, L. (Eds.). (2012). *Patterns of a network economy*. Springer Science & Business Media

Joyce, P. J., Finnveden, G., Håkansson, C., & Wood, R. (2019). A multi-impact analysis of changing ICT consumption patterns for Sweden and the EU: Indirect rebound effects and evidence of decoupling. *Journal of Cleaner Production*, *211*, 1154–1161.

Katz, M. L., & Shapiro, C. (1985). Network externalities, competition, and compatibility. *The American Economic Review*, *75*(3), 424–440.

Klimas, P., Czakon, W., Kraus, S., Kailer, N., & Maalaoui, A. (2021). Entrepreneurial failure: A synthesis and conceptual framework of its effects. *European Management Review*, *18*(1), 167–182.

Kucharska, W., Flisikowski, K., & Confente, I. (2018). Do global brands contribute to the economy of their country of origin? A dynamic spatial approach. *Journal of Product and Brand Management*, *27*(7), 768–780.

Lingo, E. L. (2023). Digital curation and creative brokering: Managing information overload in open organizing. *Organization Studies*, *44*(1), 105–133.

Livingstone, S. (2012). Critical reflections on the benefits of ICT in education. *Oxford Review of Education*, *38*(1), 9–24.

Loh, Y. A. C., & Chib, A. (2019). Tackling social inequality in development: Beyond access to appropriation of ICTs for employability. *Information Technology for Development*, *25*(3), 532–551.

Luedicke, M. K., Husemann, K. C., Furnari, S., & Ladstaetter, F. (2017). Radically open strategizing: How the premium cola collective takes open strategy to the extreme. *Long Range Planning*, *50*(3), 371–384.

Lyon, D. (2013). *The information society: Issues and illusions*. John Wiley & Sons.

Marewski, J. N., Bröder, A., & Glöckner, A. (2018). Some metatheoretical reflections on adaptive decision making and the strategy selection problem. *Journal of Behavioral Decision Making*, *31*(2), 181–198.

Martin, W. J. (2017). *The global information society*. Taylor & Francis.

Mossberger, K., Tolbert, C. J., & McNeal, R. S. (2007). *Digital citizenship: The Internet, society, and participation*. MIT Press.

Nair, M., Pradhan, R. P., & Arvin, M. B. (2020). Endogenous dynamics between R&D, ICT and economic growth: Empirical evidence from the OECD countries. *Technology in Society*, *62*, 101315.

Pike, A. (2009). Brand and branding geographies. *Geography Compass*, *3*(1), 190–213.

Pike, A. (2015). *Origination: The geographies of brands and branding*. John Wiley and Sons.

Rodríguez-Crespo, E., & Martínez-Zarzoso, I. (2019). The effect of ICT on trade: Does product complexity matter?. *Telematics and Informatics*, *41*, 182–196.

Seidl, D., Von Krogh, G. E. O. R. G., & Whittington, R. (2019). Defining open strategy: Dimensions, practices, impacts, and perspectives. In *Cambridge handbook of open strategy* (pp. 9–26). Cambridge University Press.

Tchamyou, V. S., Asongu, S. A., & Odhiambo, N. M. (2019). The role of ICT in modulating the effect of education and lifelong learning on income inequality and economic growth in Africa. *African Development Review*, *31*(3), 261–274.

Tchamyou, V. S., Erreygers, G., & Cassimon, D. (2019). Inequality, ICT and financial access in Africa. *Technological Forecasting and Social Change*, *139*, 169–184.

Van Dijk, J. (2020). *The network society*. Sage Publications.

Von Krogh, G., & Geilenger, N. (2019). Open innovation and open strategy: Epistemic and design dimensions. *Cambridge handbook of open strategy* (pp. 41–58). Cambridge University Press.

Vu, K., Hanafizadeh, P., & Bohlin, E. (2020). ICT as a driver of economic growth: A survey of the literature and directions for future research. *Telecommunications Policy*, *44*(2), 101922.

Whittington, R. (2019). *Opening strategy: Professional strategists and practice change, 1960 to today*. Oxford University Press.

Whittington, R., Cailluet, L., & Yakis-Douglas, B. (2011). Opening strategy: Evolution of a precarious profession. *British Journal of Management*, *22*(3), 531–544.

2 Open strategizing

2.1 Conceptual roots

The open strategy concept has been introduced by Chesbrough and Appleyard (2007), who were the first authors to call this approach a vital trigger in making strategic sense of innovation communities, ecosystems, and networks. Thus, the open strategy was conceptually located as an integrative component and missing link that blends already-established concepts. Considering the theoretical foundations, open strategy emerged as several scholars challenged the well-developed Porterian view on business strategy (Lerner & Tirole, 2002; West & Gallagher, 2006), but also other traditional well-established viewpoints of top management exclusivity and locus of control (Chandler, 1962) and preferring scarcity over division of resources expanded in the RBV (Barney, 1991). Finally, there was also a managerial standpoint that initiated the open strategy development as the rigid settings, with a clear division of traditionally secret and exclusive processes of strategy-making, were no longer valid (Birkinshaw, 2017). The need for greater inclusion that replaced the limited information naturally enforced the demand for a better-grounded theoretical understanding of injecting openness into strategy.

However, some attempts to increase openness in strategic issues have been made earlier. Jack Stack (1994) introduced the concept of open-book management, where the employees get insights into the strategic plans, financial documents, and strategy implementation that are fully transparent. Moreover, decision-making, power delegation, and decentralized strategy creation were also discussed (Andersen, 2004) and set the foundations for shifting the already-established concepts. Various works neglected the hegemony of managers blended with the lack of involvement of employees in strategy creation (Covin et al., 2006; Laine & Vaara, 2007) and called for greater internal inclusion and enhanced knowledge creation in the organization (Floyd & Lane, 2000). Still, there was no consensus among researchers as to the extent to engage internal stakeholders in the strategizing process (Floyd & Wooldridge, 2000), mainly because greater participation changes the balance of force and influence in the organization (Steger & Hartz, 2008). On the other hand, the

DOI: 10.4324/9781003424772-2

necessity to introduce internal clear and transparent rules, indicators, and procedures has been outlined (Mantere & Vaar, 2008). Thus, the necessity to advance the research on opening up strategic ventures has become apparent from various prospects, although it has not been fully labelled as an open strategy at that time.

To fully understand the open strategy concept, it is necessary to outline the lack of terminological purity. Scholars offered a variety of concepts concerning OS; however, not all of them are particularly different. Some embrace the same concept under different terminology, while some are only variants of other concepts. For research on the OS to be further advanced, firstly, there is a need to clarify the commonalities and differences among all relevant concepts. In some cases, open strategy is defined using content lenses, where the term is introduced as it was one of the strategy types, which may be misleading. Thus, as outlined by Kornberger (2022), there might be an impression that the narrative of open strategy is linear from closed to open, which can suggest the shift from good to better. Even the term as a noun suggests embracing another ambiguous typology of strategy types. Hence, the original intention introduced by Chesbrough and Appleyard (2007) who focused on the content view of OS has been revised in further research but not always received enough conceptual attention.

A more complex, processual view on open strategy has been introduced and developed by Whittington and colleagues (2011) who paid attention to the practices that shape the open strategy notion. The other perspective brings a more dynamic, processual approach where the shift goes to the systems used to formulate and implement the strategy in a participatory way, where both internal and external actors are involved, and the internal as well as external transparency is enhanced (Whittington et al., 2011). Such an approach has been further expanded, and the context of practices has been used to define open strategy as 'a dynamic bundle of practices' (Seidl et al., 2019) which brings the interpretation of this term more combinatory sense. As this bundle of practices may change over time and context, the authors propose to focus the definition on fundamental principles of transparency and inclusion as the features that shape those practices. Yet, the bundle suggests that there is content that integrates the actions undertaken in a strategy-making process. That is a standpoint far from the classical view on the strategy's core origins (Porter, 1980), even though the classical definition that perceived strategy as *'an abstract concept'* (Ansoff, 1988) has received some criticism and has been further verified. Thus, as already mentioned, using the term open strategy may suggest the content approach and lead to confusion that open strategy is an effect of actions and decisions undertaken to gain a competitive advantage and must be carefully addressed while using this notion.

What needs to be outlined is that it is possible to switch between closeness and openness, and thus, another feature of open strategy has to be investigated – its dynamics, as various forces cause strategic choices, and the strategic approach may evolve over time (Appleyard & Chesbrough, 2017) and expose a diversified degree of openness, making the open strategy concept 'neither absolute nor binary' (Cai & Canales, 2022, p. 16).

Addressing the dynamics of open strategy blended with the processual and content perspectives makes the research on open strategy incoherent. Some authors investigate open strategy formulation, focusing their attention on the process characteristics, describing it as collaborative, engaging, and multifaceted (Stieger et al., 2012). However, the vital query concerns the scope of the process. The formulation is a very limited view and does not fully depict the full picture. Thus, using the term open strategizing more accurately addresses the core concept. Indeed, multiple researchers have already discussed the practices and activities used within strategizing processes (Jarzabkowski, 2008; Jarzabkowski & Balogun, 2009; Mantere & Vaara, 2008) and the strategy-as-practice stream of research (Vaara & Whittington, 2012) has gained recently more attention. Those practices are defined very broadly as they cover a range of diversified activities and shared routines of behaviour (Paroutis & Pettigrew, 2007; Whittington, 2006) and are not limited to managers only. Thus, concentrating scholars' attention on open strategizing brings more clarity to further theorizing.

To enhance conceptual clarity, it is worth investigating the relationship between open strategy and open strategizing to uncover whether open strategizing could be a central concept used further, as it seems a necessary condition to discuss open strategy (perceived more like an outcome of applying the processual view). That is the main logic we follow in this book, as we want to focus our attention on the process (strategizing), not its effect. Thus, we assume that open strategizing is an essential notion that leads to developing an open strategy perceived as a consequence of applying the open approach in the strategy-making process. Hence, it is not vital to consider the strategy type itself but to focus on leading practices, which is a core standpoint of the strategy-as-practice view (Kohtamäki et al., 2022). It has been recently outlined by Splitter et al. (2023), who indicate a limited understanding of openness and applying disjoint perspectives of separate investigations. Authors call for a more integrated perception of openness within organizational domains and call it open organizing. However, such a standpoint of open organizing allocates attention to the operational, not strategical, view, and we decide to use the term open strategizing to fully reflect the investigated phenomenon. We perceive open strategizing using dynamic lenses as the 'flow of actions and interactions' (Jarzabkowski et al., 2019, p. 854) aimed to bring transparency and inclusiveness into the strategizing process (Weiser et al., 2020) with a central role of practitioners and practices.

In the next sections, we will briefly discuss the previous research streams with their limitations to bring more clarity into the open strategizing research avenues. Extent analysis of previous works enabled us to recognize four main domains where the scholars' attention is located. We perceive applying open strategizing as a setting that may ultimately lead to having an open strategy, resulting in various benefits and challenges that naturally emerge. However, as it is not required to reveal the final decisions fully, and various, diversified facets may form the strategy concepts, open strategizing may finally lead to the partial or limited announcement of the implemented direction of development. As an open strategy is not a goal *per se*, it should not be treated as one of the managerial choices regarding the strategy type implemented in the organization. Stjerne et al. (2022) claim that we may observe a 'strategic practice drift', where some gradual and partly unnoticed shifts toward open strategy may be applied in the organization. If so, the open practices may even be not recognized but form an integral part of organizational DNA. Thus, using the term open strategizing would better fit this complex concept.

Applying the processual view as a main standpoint results in recognizing four main domains that contribute to understanding open strategizing: the perception of this concept, the driving forces that trigger the open strategizing practices, the methods that are used to shape those practices, and finally – the practitioners that are involved. The following sections bring insights to delineate and understand those four themes.

2.2   Open strategizing perception

Perception of open strategizing has some common ground with the open innovation (OI) concept, as in both cases, the external inspirations are absorbed (Chesbrough, 2003a), and the flow of inbound and outgoing information spreads (Bogers et al., 2018) within the organization, and its ecosystem (Costa et al., 2023). Moreover, in both concepts, knowledge, technology, and resources drift beyond the organizational boundaries (Clegg et al., 2019), but also the internal ideas are applied and considered (Dahlander & Piezunka, 2014; Chiaroni et al., 2011). Thanks to the ongoing process of information and communications technology development, companies' challenges may be diffused externally, and they receive diversified insights that contribute to both open innovation and open strategizing (Bogers et al., 2018). With the rapid evolution of technology, a shift towards core competitive skills of critical thinking and creativity (Javaid & Haleem, 2020) also fosters the development of both concepts, as those skills can, or even must be, externally possessed. Finally, both concepts aim to advance the innovation process (Enkel et al., 2009) despite that the scope, complexity, and dispersion of participants in those processes are permanently evolving (Chesbrough, 2019). However, open strategizing, contrary to OI, which aims to blend external and internal ideas to progress innovations (Bogers et al., 2019), is not devoted only to innovation but has a more compound nature. Moreover, the main difference that occurs is the shift towards a sensemaking process, which is definitely the open strategizing domain (Schmitt, 2010), as well as individual empowerment vital for enhancing the commitment to strategy (Nketia, 2016).

Although the grounds and roots of open strategizing have already been outlined in other research, the perception of this concept has still rather fluid boundaries, making it blurry and difficult to delineate from other organizational praxis explicitly. Thus, no measures have been developed so far. Some attempts to measure the concept of open strategy have been made by Pittz and Adler (2023), who refined and validated this construct and set some empirical grounding. Yet, it is neither conceptually, nor empirically, established how to address the measurement of transparency and inclusiveness with the constraints and profits that may occur. There is also a lack of diversification between external and internal perspectives, or long- versus short-term approaches. However, without any doubts, both – the benefits and challenges of open strategizing – are hindered or boosted by the actions undertaken by the practitioners. Their open strategizing perception impacts the adoption or rejection of particular practices, as well as the comprehensive or partial acceptance and finally – involvement.

There are several reasons why open strategizing is perceived as being in constant flux. The first one is the evolving and transformative organizational context where open practices that have an impact on perception shaping are adopted (Smith et al., 2018). The other reason is the limited attention of actors that need to share their attention between various initiatives and may overlook the priorities when the attention structures collide (Brielmaier & Friesl, 2023). Finally, because of the non-binary character of openness, it should not be analyzed dichotomously with the distinction between absolute openness versus closeness (Ates, 2019). Instead, it is portrayed as a continuum of varying degrees of openness with various temporal elements and evolving praxis with no rigid boundaries and no fixed timelines.

The dimensionality of this construct also has an impact on the fluidity of the open strategizing construct. The understanding of open strategizing has always been conceptualized by two dimensions: inclusiveness and transparency. The first one covers the practices of broadening the range of actors (Kennedy et al., 2016; Pittz & Adler, 2016) and the second one – the visibility of data being communicated (Appleyard & Chesbrough, 2017; Gegenhuber & Dobusch, 2017).

In the case of transparency, procedural transparency (contextual, embedded in the strategic processes) and transparency of the participants' assets or resources must be conceptually delineated (Cai & Canales, 2022). Thus, diversified actors and practices are employed, depending on the scope and type of data revealed. While defining inclusion, it is vital to distinguish inclusion from participation as it explains the continuum between fully open and fully closed strategizing (Mack & Szulanski, 2017). That distinction is based on passing the power, control, and responsibility – that is, more of an inclusive nature rather than restraining the contribution to information delivery and providing solutions to already-defined problems – which is participatory (Mantere, 2008). Delineating the inclusion from participation brings more clarity when analyzing the nature of open strategizing practices and their outcomes (Jarzabkowski et al., 2016). Employing inclusion means developing inclusive practices where various actors are engaged not only to consult but also to create, shape, inspire, and even decide about strategic initiatives.

Although much has been written about those two open strategizing dimensions (Schnackenberg & Tomlinson, 2016; Merlo et al., 2018; Holland et al., 2018; Whitehurst, 2015; Barroso-Castro et al., 2017; Aten & Thomas, 2016), the investigation of their mutual relations is still scarce. Still, it has not been fully evident whether it is necessary or even possible to address at the same time full transparency with broad inclusiveness. In fact, such an approach may be utopic, as the practitioners (discussed further in this chapter) may not have the ability or willingness to interact with the organization, and, at the same time, extensive transparency may not be needed, desired, or expected.

Besides transparency and inclusion, some scholars pay attention to the third, commonly under-investigated in the OS stream of research (Morton et al., 2019) – the dimension of IT enablers introduced by Tavakoli et al. (2015) that may be perceived as a facilitator of the intertwined relations between other two dimensions. The mediating role of technology in communication between various actors definitely enhanced the possibilities of inclusion of the practitioners beyond the organization (Haefliger, 2019). Digital technologies naturally shifted the types of interactions vital for open strategizing (Majchrzak & Malhotra, 2013; Baptista et al., 2017) and supported co-creation practices (Doeleman et al., 2022). Analog interactions have been replaced by blogs, online platforms, jamming, social bookmarking (Giuffrida & Dittrich, 2013), and other forms of digital communication highly boosted by social media development (Rottner et al., 2019) and even called social software (Shirky, 2005) – a group of applications used to strategy shaping activities (Haefliger et al., 2011). Such a shift resulted in a change in the social relationships network (Hautz, 2019) by shaping daily interactions (Neeley & Leonardi, 2018), impacting both the transparency and inclusiveness dimensions in their scope and form. As claimed by Heracleous (2019) *'dialogic and open strategy processes are contingent, context-embedded, and context-dependent'*. Thus, further research in the digitalization context is justified.

2.3   Open strategizing triggers

There are no established categories of open strategizing triggers, perceived as a stimuli, that would facilitate the development of open practices, either temporarily or permanently. Based on the conceptual investigation of the activators discussed in the open strategy stream of research, two main perspectives may be discussed: driving forces (the circumstances and the nature of drivers that endorse injecting openness) and conditions (the features of the environment where those practices emerge).

The driving forces are the motives for enhancing openness in strategizing and may be internal (voluntary) or external (imposed for various reasons). The external triggers result from the growing public expectations regarding organizational transparency on the one hand and declining trust in data reliability on the other hand, which leads to rising organizational tensions between fitting into the expected standard of internal information sharing and keeping control (Heimstädt, 2017). Moreover, the openness may be transferred from the encompassing network of stakeholders such as consultants, state agencies, media, business schools (Vaara & Whittington, 2012), customers, or scientists (Aten & Thomas, 2016) that interlay their practices and pass over their meanings, interpretations, and expectations. Although those practices are being externally passed on, the need to develop open practices may be internally inspired. The growing complexity of organizational difficulties intensifies the efforts to gain some interorganizational stimulation that may be derived from strategic alliances, partnerships, coalitions, or originate from the actual involvement in the business ecosystems (Wulf & Butel, 2016; Seidl & Werle, 2018). Thus, the external facilitators of open strategizing may have diversified origins, ranging from the pressure of disclosure, the burden of delving into the network, or the need to comply with the standards set by the organization's stakeholders.

The internal drivers have more institutional facets, including predefined awareness of strategy actors and sensegiving efforts that emerge within the organization (Goldenstein & Walgenbach, 2019). Moreover, the informal interactions and relational interplay, being supported by social technology, foster information flow and bidirectional communication (Stieger et al., 2012; Baptista et al., 2017). Hence, the internal facilitators are more voluntary and emerge naturally from the organizational routines or their amendments.

Recognizing the impact of internal and external triggers is valuable to understand how open strategizing is employed and whether it is a forced reaction or appears naturally. In fact, the dichotomy of applying transparency has already been recognized and categorized as instrumental (used to pursue a goal) or purposeful (used to pursue a natural willingness to be open) (Baraibar-Diez et al., 2017). Thus, the context plays a pivotal role (Lee & Comello, 2019) and needs to be considered, as inclusiveness and transparency are not the aims per se but may evolve over time and emerge as a response to various triggers.

Besides the external or internal triggers of open strategizing, scholars pay attention to the conditions where the openness is developed, which may enhance or hinder emerging open practices. One type of activator that emerges in the environment is social media usage as a tool for developing those practices. In fact, as outlined recently by Henriksson and Sorsa (2023), inclusion is not always planned but may emerge intrinsically, bringing uncontrolled dynamics of inclusion and transparency and then being orchestrated by the organization. Such unrestrained facilitators bring even more complexity to managerial challenges as the need for moderating the unintended but essential forum for open strategizing becomes serious and may not be ignored.

Open strategizing has been activated by the possibilities created by digital and virtual spaces as they reduced structural and social barriers to openness and boosted the possibilities of idea development (Mount et al., 2020) as well as unlashed the flow of knowledge sharing, including the competences and experiences (Faraj et al., 2016). However, the involvement of virtual spaces is not so straightforward as a mismatch with more traditional forms of organizing has also been reported (Kornberger et al., 2017). In fact, as recently shown by Holstein and Rantakari (2023), space needs to be perceived as an important trigger of openness as it impacts the dynamics of openness and may turn disclosure into closure. The authors mention three spatial features – physical visibility, strategizing artefact, and discursive designation as the pivotal openness facilitators (or constraints). Thus, although the motives are vital to understand the dynamics of open strategizing, the space and creating a suitable environment are also essential as they may finally activate and blend openness into organizational practice.

2.4   Open strategizing practices

As open strategizing is perceived as a bunch of practices, it is vital to understand how to develop acceptance for enhancing transparency and inclusiveness and what methods could be used to support those practices. There are numerous divisions of transparency practices. First, the practices differ regarding the process timing. Transparency can be applied during the ideation phase when the strategic direction is shaped and communicated (Tackx & Verdin, 2014;) or during the strategy execution (Matzler et al.,2014). Second, practices differ regarding the scope of information that is revealed as it may cover strategic information (Baptista et al., 2017), strategic projects (Appleyard & Chesbrough, 2017), implementation of strategic ventures (Newstead & Lanzerotti, 2010), or some public, externally driven, announcements of strategic cooperation (i.e., mergers and acquisitions) (Yakis-Douglas et al., 2017). Finally, the transparency practices may be voluntary, mandatory, or pressured by nonlegal or nonregulatory forces. The last type of enforced practice is called disruptive tactics imposed by the demanding stakeholders with limited involvement in the strategy-making who exert pressure to reveal the strategic information (Ohlson & Yakis-Douglas, 2019). The practices also cover prioritizing relevant data over the one that cannot or does not need to be revealed (Whittington et al., 2011), leading to concealing other information (Fenster, 2015).

Regarding inclusiveness, crowdsourcing is the most commonly reported practice (Amrollahi & Ghapnchi, 2016; Afuah & Tucci, 2012), as well as dialoguing, defined as communicative interactions (Heracleous, 2019). In fact, the range of options differs regarding their form. In the case of analog, more traditional practices are developed, and researchers report workshops, town halls, World Cafés or surveys, and in digital forms, the range of practices is broader, including wikis, blogs, and web-based crowdsourcing (Hautz et al., 2019).

When it comes to investigating the methods used to inject openness, some exemplary initiatives have already been identified. We may mention one-page visual strategy maps, already-explored conceptions like Balanced Scorecard, EFQM, Hoshin Kanri (Hoque, 2014; Tortorella et al., 2018). Such formalized methods have been extensively used internally in organizations, but they bring only partial value as the core locus of their usage is on monitoring goal achievement (Tezel et al., 2016) and not on the complex strategizing process. Thus, their focus is more on the effect, not how it is achieved. Employment of those methods is a part of organizational practices that would transform how they are perceived and their role in the open strategizing.

A limited discussion on how to address transparency and inclusion simultaneously has been developed so far. Indeed, in most cases, only one of the dimensions is referred to. Some attempts were made to conceptually integrate those dimensions to differentiate the transparency practices regarding the collective or individual perspective of analysis (Baraibar-Diez et al., 2017). Such variation is based on the participatory dichotomy and brings inclusiveness into consideration. However, external and internal expectations (Rawlins, 2009) impact the relationship between transparent and inclusive practices. The mismatch between what is needed and what is delivered may boost or hinder the development of organizational practices.

While discussing open strategizing practices, attention should be paid to the relation between inclusion and exclusion, which may fluctuate and evolve due to social and organizational practices limiting participation (Vaara et al., 2019). This view is rooted in the belief that strategic actors develop specific practices due to some circumstances and that organizations hold a bundle of reactively used practices (Splitter et al., 2019). However, all those practices require reflexiveness, which emerges to bridge the tensions arising from the participatory nature of intensified digitalization and existing management practices (Baptista et al., 2017).

Wawarta and Paroutis (2019) have distinguished two emerging practices that may be classified as top-down deductive or bottom-up inductive practices of open strategizing. Various challenges may impose the need to employ those practices otherwise to overcome the linguistic and conceptual impediments. Those practices are labelled as open but do not specifically address transparency and/or inclusiveness as open strategizing dimensions. Instead, they are rather intuitive and based on reflexive responses to the emerging need to address the arising challenges. Thus, the need to investigate the relations between transparency and inclusion practices as well as their dynamics exposed by the combinations of openness and closure in strategy-making process is postulated (Dobusch & Dobusch, 2019), making exploring open strategizing practices an entangled problem.

2.5   Open strategizing practitioners

The role of practitioners is twofold. First, they represent the practices existing within the organization. Second, they transfer the external practices from outside the organization and use them further in strategizing (Splitter et al., 2019). As a result, many bundled practices are created and used contextually by practitioners who implement them in particular organizational settings. What is also important is the sensegiving trait that affects personal interpretations (Bowman, 2016) and shapes the practices. As a result, sensegiving may strengthen or oppose the open strategizing dimensions (Bencherki et al., 2019). As this process is highly individualized, it may trigger rising tensions. Regarding transparency, diverse standpoints may emerge as the perspective of concealing or revealing the information may have varied personal origins. In the case of inclusiveness, the individual sense of commitment is crucial. Thus, transmitting the meaning over the organization is not reduced to specific groups of practitioners but has a more collective nature where differing goals and interests must be considered (Bencherki et al., 2019). It is even more complex when the external actors are to be considered, as their involvement changes the established roles and procedures (Alexy et al., 2013). Therefore, there is a call for more advanced research on fluid organization structures that balance and integrate those dispersed perspectives (Majchrzak et al., 2018). The claim to '*identify when, how, and why it would be beneficial to engage in open strategizing*' (Xu & Alexy, 2019, p. 71) remains relevant from the practitioners' perspective. As outlined by Luedicke and colleagues (2017), even in the case of radically open strategizing, when there is a willingness to reveal a broad range of information rather than exclude some actors, the limitations come from the participants who selectively use the opportunities of employing the open strategizing practices. Thus, among the research results developed so far, we may certainly indicate the role of actors who are engaged in open strategizing practices, but there are no methods or tools to measure organizational or individual readiness to open up the strategizing process. As already discussed in Section 1.3, it may be voluntary or forced and those two types of triggers would also impact the readiness. Finally, the external perspective of practitioners is also under-investigated, as there are fundamental questions that need to be addressed – that is, is involving the client in the project enough to call it an open strategizing practice or how to balance confidentiality with disclosure and recognize the potential readiness of external actors. Those are just exemplary queries that need to be tackled in further research.

The vital theme that needs to be addressed is the question of who should be involved and to what extent the knowledge should be revealed to various actors (Mirabeau & Maguire, 2014; Hautz et al., 2017). Two main risks occur while the broader inclusion is employed. One are the knowledge gaps developed when there is a mismatch between listening, understanding, or integrating each other's knowledge (Cronin & Weingart, 2007). Those gaps become apparent in all three settings: between the external actors, across the internal and external actors, as well as between internal members, and lead to weakening the novelty of strategic suggestions (Marabelli & Newell, 2012) and failure of solutions implementation (Denyer et al., 2011).

The other risk, although related to the knowledge gaps, is more interest-based. Actors engaged in open strategizing may reveal contentious and opposing interests over resources and directions or prioritize their own purposes (Malhotra et al., 2017). Thus, the pivotal question is how to identify valuable, relevant, and strategically aware actors (Matzler et al., 2016). What brings more complexity to this challenge is the fact that some of the selected participants may be more critically important than others (Hautz, 2019). Identification and engagement of those practitioners would enhance the quality of applied practices.

Various researchers have already outlined the value of opening up (Chesbrough, 2003; von Hippel, 2005) as the potential outcomes are straightforward to be recognized. Starting from the information access and knowledge flow (Amrollahi & Rowlands, 2017), improving the implementation effects (Stieger et al., 2012), increasing the strategic identity (Morton et al., 2018), boosted commitment (Lakhani et al., 2013) and finally – leading to emergence of unexpected and extraordinary solutions and recognized skills (Whittington, 2019). Regarding the external outcomes of open strategizing, we may mention its effect on crafting the corporate reputation (Martens et al., 2007) and using it as a part of impression management, shaping the perception of the external audience (Gegenhuber & Dobusch, 2017). Much has also been written about the potential challenges that may occur: the risk of intended or unintended revealing the sensitive information (Mack & Szulanski, 2017), involuntary need to impose openness (Nason et al., 2018), blurring priorities (von Hippel & von Krogh, 2016), enhancing the commitment (Neeley & Leonardi, 2018), or overcoming the organizational obstacles (Radomska et al., 2023). Yet, finding the balance between dealing with those challenges and obtaining the required level of openness must be addressed by core organizational policy makers.

References

Afuah, A., & Tucci, C. (2012). Crowdsourcing as a solution to distant search. *Academy of Management Review*, *37*(3), 355–375.
Alexy, O., Henkel, J., & Wallin, M. W. (2013). From closed to open: Job role changes, individual predispositions, and the adoption of commercial open sources of software development. *Research Policy*, *42*(8), 1325–1340.
Amrollahi, A., & Ghapnchi, A. H. (2016). Open strategic planning in universities: A case study. In T. X. Bui & R. H. Sprague, Jr. (Eds.), *HICSS 2016:*

Proceedings of the 49th annual Hawaii international conference on system sciences (pp. 386–395). Institute of Electrical and Electronics Engineers (IEEE)

Amrollahi, A., & Rowlands, B. (2017). Collaborative open strategic planning: A method and case study. *Information Technology & People, 30*(4), 832–852.

Andersen, T. J. (2004). Integrating decentralized strategy making and strategic planning processes in dynamic environments. *Journal of Management Studies, 41*, 1271–1299.

Ansoff, I. (1988). *New corporate strategy*. John Wiley & Sons.

Appleyard, M., & Chesbrough, H. (2017). The dynamics of open strategy: From adoption to reversion. *Long Range Planning, 50*, 310–321.

Aten, K., & Thomas, G. F. (2016). Crowdsourcing strategizing: Communication technology affordances and the communicative constitution of organizational strategy. *International Journal of Business Communication, 53*(2), 148–180.

Ates, A. (2019). Exploring adaptive small and medium enterprises through the lens of open strategy. In T. J. Andersen, S. Torp & S. Linder (Eds.), *Strategic responsiveness and adaptive organizations: New research frontiers in international strategic management* (pp. 25–39). (Emerald Studies in Global Strategic Responsiveness), Emerald Publishing Limited.

Baptista, J., Wilson, A., Galliers, R., & Bynghall, S. (2017). Social media and the emergence of reflexiveness as a new capability for open strategy. *Long Range Planning, 50*(3), 322–336.

Baraibar-Diez, E., Odriozola, M. D., & Fernández Sánchez, J. L. (2017). A Survey of transparency: An intrinsic aspect of business strategy. *Business Strategy and the Environment, 26*, 480–489.

Barney, J. (1991). Firm resources and sustained competitive advantage. *Journal of Management, 17*(1), 99–120.

Barroso-Castro, C., Villegas-Periñan, M. M., & Dominguez, M. (2017). Board members' contribution to strategy: The mediating role of board internal processes. *European Research on Management and Business Economics, 23*(2), 82–89.

Bencherki, N., Basque, J., & Rouleau, L. (2019). A sensemaking perspective on open strategy. In D. Seidl, G. Von Krogh & R. Whittington (Eds.), *Cambridge handbook of open strategy* (pp. 241–258). Cambridge University Press.

Birkinshaw, J. (2017). Reflections on open strategy. *Long Range Planning, 50*(3), 423–426.

Bogers, M., Chesbrough, H., & Moedas, C. (2018). Open innovation: Research, practices, and policies. *California Management Review, 60*(2), 5–16.

Bogers, M., Chesbrough, H., Heaton, S., & Teece, D. J. (2019). Strategic management of open innovation: A dynamic capabilities perspective. *California Management Review, 62*(1), 77–94.

Bowman, G. (2016). The practice of scenario planning: an analysis of inter- and intra-organizational strategizing. *British Journal of Management, 27*(1), 77–96.

Brielmaier, C., & Friesl, M. (2023). Pulled in all directions: Open strategy participation as an attention contest. *Strategic Organization, 21*(3), 709–720.

Cai, J., & Canales, J. (2022). Dual strategy process in open strategizing. *Long Range Planning, 55.*

Chandler, A. (1962). Strategy and structure: Chapters in the history of the American enterprise. *Massachusetts Institute of Technology Cambridge, 4*(2), 125–137.

Chesbrough, H. (2003a). *Open innovation: The new imperative for creating and profiting from technology.* Harvard Business School Press.

Chesbrough, H. (2003b). The logic of open innovation: Managing intellectual property. *California Management Review, 45*(3), 33–58.

Chesbrough, H. (2019). *Open innovation results: Going beyond the hype and getting down to business* (1st ed.). Oxford University Press.

Chesbrough, H. W., & Appleyard, M. M. (2007). Open innovation and strategy. *California Management Review, 50*(1), 57–76.

Chiaroni, D., Chiesa, V., & Frattini, F. (2011). The open innovation journey: How firms dynamically implement the emerging innovation management paradigm. *Technovation, 31*(1), 34–43.

Clegg, S., Van Rijmenam, M., & Schweitzer, J. (2019). The politics of openness. In D. Seidl, G. Von Krogh & R. Whittington (Eds.), *Cambridge handbook of open strategy* (pp. 307–325). Cambridge University Press.

Costa, J., Amorim, I., Reis, J., & Melão, N. (2023). User communities: From nice-to-have to must-have. *Journal of Innovation and Entrepreneurship, 12*(25).

Covin, J. G., Green, K. M., & Slevin, D. P. (2006). Strategic process effects on the entrepreneurial orientation-sales growth rate relationship. *Entrepreneurship Theory and Practice, 30*(1), 57–81.

Cronin, M., & Weingart, L. (2007). Representational gaps, information processing, and conflicting functionally diverse teams. *Academy of Management Review, 32*(3), 761–773.

Dahlander, L., & Piezunka, H. (2014). Open to suggestions: How organizations elicit suggestions through proactive and reactive attention. *Research Policy, 43*(5), 812–827.

Denyer, D., Parry, E., & Flowers, P. (2011). "Social", "open" and "participative"? Exploring personal experiences and organizational effects of enterprise 2.0 use. *Long Range Planning, 44*(5), 375–396.

Dobusch, L., & Dobusch, L. (2019). The relation between openness and closure in open strategy: Programmatic and constitutive approaches to openness. In D. Seidl, G. Von Krogh & R. Whittington (Eds.), *Cambridge handbook of open strategy* (pp. 326–336). Cambridge University Press.

Doeleman, H. J., van Dun, D. H., & Wilderom, C. P. M. (2022). Leading open strategizing practices for effective strategy implementation. *Journal of Strategy and Management, 15*(1), 54–75.

Enkel, E., Gassmann, O., & Chesbrough, H. (2009). Open R&D and open innovation: Exploring the phenomenon. *R&D Management, 39*(4), 311–316.

Faraj, S., von Krogh, G., Monteiro, E., & Lakhani, K. (2016). Special section introduction – Online community as space for knowledge flows. *Information Systems Research, 27*, 668–684.

Fenster, M. (2015). Transparency in search of a theory. *European Journal of Social Theory, 18*(2), 150–167.

Floyd, S., & Lane, P. (2000). Strategizing throughout the organization: Managing role of conflict in strategic renewal. *Academy of Management Review,* (25), 156.

Floyd, S., & Wooldridge, B. (2000). *Building strategy from the middle* (p. 134). Sage Publications.

Gegenhuber, T., & Dobusch, L. (2017). Making an impression through openness: How open strategy-making practices change in the evolution of new ventures. *Long Range Planning, 50*(3), 337–354.

Giuffrida, R., & Dittrich, Y. (2013). Empirical studies on the use of social software in global software development – A systematic mapping study. *Information and Software Technology, 55*(7), 1143–1164.

Goldenstein, J., & Walgenbach, P. (2019). An institutional perspective on open strategy: Strategy in world society. In *Cambridge handbook of open strategy* (pp. 289–303). Cambridge University Press.

Haefliger, S. (2019). Orientations of open strategy: From resistance to transformation. In D. Seidl, G. Von Krogh & R. Whittington (Eds.), *Cambridge handbook of open strategy* (pp. 151–166). Cambridge University Press.

Haefliger, S., Monteiro, E., Foray, D., & von Krogh, G. (2011). Social software and strategy. *Long Range Planning, 44*(5–6), 297–316.

Hautz, J. (2019). A social network perspective on open strategy. In D. Seidl, G. Von Krogh & R. Whittington (Eds.), *Cambridge handbook of open strategy* (pp. 272–288). Cambridge University Press.

Hautz, J., Seidl, D., & Whittington, R. (2017). Open strategy: Dimensions, dilemmas, dynamics. *Long Range Planning, 50*(3), 298–309.

Hautz, J., Hutter, K., & Sutter, J. (2019). Practices of inclusion in open strategy. In D. Seidl, G. von Krogh & R. Whittington (Eds.), *Cambridge handbook of open strategy* (pp. 87–105). Cambridge University Press.

Heimstädt, M. (2017). Openwashing: A decoupling perspective on organizational transparency. *Technological Forecasting and Social Change, 125*, 77–86.

Henriksson, E., & Sorsa, V. (2023). Open strategizing on social media: A process model of emotional mechanisms and outcomes from un-orchestrated participation. *Long Range Planning, 56*(3).

Heracleous, L. (2019). A dialogic perspective on open strategy. In *Cambridge handbook of open strategy* (pp. 259–271). Cambridge University Press.

Holstein, J., & Rantakari, A. (2023). Space and the dynamic between openness and closure: Open strategizing in the TV series Borgen. *Organization Studies, 44*(1), 53–75.

Holland, D., Krause, A., Provencher, J., & Seltzer, T. (2018). Transparency tested: The influence of message features on public perceptions of organizational transparency. *Public Relations Review, 44*(2), 256–264.

Hoque, Z. (2014). 20 years of studies on the balanced scorecard: Trends, accomplishments, gaps and opportunities for future research. *The British Accounting Review, 46*(1), 33–59.

Jarzabkowski, P. (2008). Shaping strategy as a structuration process. *Academy of Management Journal, 51*, 621–650.

Jarzabkowski, P., & Balogun, J. (2009). The practice and process of delivering integration through strategic planning. *Journal of Management Studies, 46*, 1255–1288.

Jarzabkowski, P., Kaplan, S., Seidl, D., & Whittington, R. (2016). On the risk of studying practices in isolation: Linking what, who, and how in strategy research. *Strategic Organization, 14*, 248–259.

Jarzabkowski, P., Le, J., & Balogun, J. (2019). The social practice of coevolving strategy and structure to realize mandated radical change. *Academy of Management Journal, 62*(3), 850–882.

Javaid, M., & Haleem, A. (2020). Critical components of Industry 5.0 towards a successful adoption in the field of manufacturing. *Journal of Industrial Integration and Management, 5*(3), 327–348.

Kennedy, S., Whiteman, G., & van den Ende, J. (2016). Radical innovation for sustainability: The power of strategy and open innovation. *Long Range Planning, 50*(6), 712–725.

Kohtamäki, M., Whittington, R., Vaara, E., & Rabetino, R. (2022). Making connections: Harnessing the diversity of strategy-as-practice research. *International Journal of Management Reviews, 24*, 210–232.

Kornberger, M. (2022). Media review: Richard Whittington, opening strategy: Professional strategists and practice change, 1960 to today. *Organization Studies, 43*(2), 314–316.

Kornberger, M., Meyer, R., Brandtner, C., & Höllerer, M. (2017). When bureaucracy meets the crowd: Studying "open government" in the Vienna city administration. *Organization Studies, 38*, 179–200.

Laine, P., & Vaara, E. (2007). Struggling over subjectivity: A discursive analysis of strategic development in an engineering group. *Human Relations*, (60), 30.

Lakhani, K., Lifshitz-Assaf, H., & Tushman, M. (2013). Open innovation and organizational boundaries: The impact of task decomposition and knowledge distribution on the locus of innovation. In A. Grandori (Ed.), *Handbook of economic organization: Integrating economic and organization theory* (pp. 355–382). Edward Elgar Publishing.

Lee, T. H., & Comello, M. L. (Nori) G. (2019). Transparency and Industry stigmatization in strategic CSR communication. *Management Communication Quarterly, 33*(1), 68–85.

Lerner, J., & Tirole, J. (2002). Some simple economics of open source. *The Journal of Industrial Economics*, (2), 197–234.

Luedicke, M., Husemann, K., Furnari, S., & Ladstaetter, F. (2017). Radically open strategizing: How the premium cola collective takes open strategy to the extreme. *Long Range Planning, 50*(3), 371–384.

Mack, D., & Szulanski, G. (2017). Opening Up: How centralization affects participation and inclusion in strategy making. *Long Range Planning, 50*, 385–396.

Majchrzak, A., Griffith, T., Reetz, D., & Alexy, O. (2018). Catalyst organizations as a new organization design for innovation: The case of hyperloop transportation technologies. *Academy of Management Discoveries, 4*(4), 472–496.

Majchrzak, A., & Malhotra, A. (2013). Towards an information systems perspective and research agenda on crowdsourcing for innovation. *The Journal of Strategic Information Systems, 22*(4), 257–268.

Malhotra, A., Majchrzak, A., & Niemiec, R. (2017). Using public crowds for open strategy formulation: Mitigating the risks of knowledge gaps. *Long Range Planning, 50*(3), 397–410.

Mantere, S. (2008). Role expectations and middle managers strategic agency. *Journal of Management Studies, 45*, 294–316.

Mantere, S., & Vaara, E. (2008). On the problem of participation in strategy: A critical discursive perspective. *Organization Science, 19*, 341–358.

Marabelli, M., & Newell, S. (2012). Knowledge risks in organizational networks: The practice perspective. *The Journal of Strategic Information Systems*, *21*(1), 18–30.

Martens, M., Jennings, J., & Jennings, P. (2007). Do the stories they tell get them the money they need? The role of entrepreneurial narratives in resource acquisition. *Academy of Management Journal*, *50*, 1107–1132.

Matzler, K., Fuller, J., Koch, B., Hautz, J., & Hutter, K. (2014). Open strategy – a new strategy paradigm? In K. Matzler, H. Pechlaner & B. Renzl (Eds.), *Strategie und leadership*. Springer Gabler.

Matzler, K., Füller, J., Hutter, K., Hautz, J., & Stieger, D. (2016). Crowdsourcing strategy: How openness changes strategy work. *Problems and Perspectives in Management*, *14*(3), 450–460.

Merlo, O., Eisingerich, A., Auh, S., & Levstek, J. (2018). The benefits and implementation of performance transparency: The why and how of letting your customers 'see through' your business. *Business Horizons*, *61*(1), 73–84.

Mirabeau, L., & Maguire, S. (2014). From autonomous strategic behaviour to emergent strategy. *Strategic Management Journal*, *35*, 1202–1229.

Morton, J., Wilson, A., & Cooke, L. (2018). Managing organizational legitimacy through modes of open strategizing. In *Academy of management proceedings. 78th annual meeting of the academy of management, 10–14 Aug 2018*. Academy of Management.

Morton, J., Wilson, A., Galliers, R. D., & Marabelli, M. (2019). Open Strategy and Information Technology. In D. Seidl, G. von Krogh, & R. Whittington (Eds.), *Cambridge Handbook of Open Strategy* (pp. 169–185). chapter, Cambridge: Cambridge University Press.

Mount, M., Clegg, S., & Pitsis, T. (2020). Conceptualizing the de-materializing characteristics of internal inclusion in crowdsourced open strategy. *Long Range Planning*, *53*, 1–10.

Nason, R. S., Bacq, S., & Gras, D. (2018). A behavioral theory of social performance: Social identity and stakeholder expectations. *Academy of Management Review*, *43*(2), 259–283.

Neeley, T., & Leonardi, P. (2018). Enacting knowledge strategy through social media: Passable trust and the paradox of nonwork interactions. *Strategic Management Journal*, *39*, 922–946.

Newstead, B., & Lanzerotti, L. (2010). Can you open source your strategy? *Harvard Business Review*. October.

Nketia, B. (2016). The influence of open strategizing on organizational members' commitment to strategy. *Procedia – Social and Behavioral Sciences*, *235*, 473–483.

Ohlson, T., & Yakis-Douglas, B. (2019). Practices of transparency in open strategy: Beyond the dichotomy of voluntary and mandatory disclosure. In D. Seidl, G. Von Krogh & R. Whittington (Eds.), *Cambridge handbook of open strategy* (pp. 136–150). Cambridge University Press.

Paroutis, S., & Pettigrew, A. (2007). Strategizing in the multi-business firm: Strategy teams at multiple levels and overtime. *Human Relations*, *60*, 99–135.

Pittz, T., & Adler, T. (2016). An exemplar of open strategy: Decision-making within multi-sector collaborations. *Management Decision*, *54*(7), 1595–1614.

Pittz, T., & Adler, T. (2023). Open strategy as a catalyst for innovation: Evidence from cross-sector social partnerships. *Journal of Business Research,* *160.*

Porter, M. E. (1980). *Competitive strategy: Techniques for analysing industries and competitors.* Free Press.

Radomska, J., Hajdas M., Wołczek P., Glinka B. (2023), Wide open? Creative industries and open strategizing challenges, *International Journal of Management and Economics, 59*(2), 117–136.

Rawlins, B. (2009). Give the emperor a mirror: Toward developing a stakeholder measurement of organizational transparency. *Journal of Public Relations Research, 21*(1), 71–99.

Rottner, R., Bovenberg, D., & Leonardi, P. (2019). Social media in open strategy: A five-flows model of strategy making and enactment. In D. Seidl, G. Von Krogh & R. Whittington (Eds.), *Cambridge handbook of open strategy* (pp. 186–204). Cambridge University Press.

Schmitt, R. (2010). Dealing with wicked issues: Open strategizing and the camisea case. *Journal of Business Ethics, 96*(1), 11–19.

Schnackenberg, A. K., & Tomlinson, E. C. (2016). Organizational transparency: A new perspective on managing trust in organization-stakeholder relationships. *Journal of Management, 42*(7), 1784–1810.

Seidl, D., Von Krogh, G., & Whittington, R. (2019). Defining open strategy: Dimensions, practices, impacts, and perspectives. In D. Seidl, G. Von Krogh & R. Whittington (Eds.), *Cambridge handbook of open strategy* (pp. 9–26). Cambridge University Press.

Seidl, D., & Werle, F. (2018). Inter-organizational sensemaking in the face of strategic meta-problems: Requisite variety and dynamics of participation. *Strategic Management Journal, 39*(3), 830–858.

Shirky, C. (2005). Group as user: Flaming and the design of social software. In *The best software writing* (pp. 183–209). Apress.

Smith, P., Callagher, L., Crewe-Brown, J., & Siedlok, F. (2018). Zones of participation (and non-participation) in open strategy: Desirable, actual and undesirable. *M@n@gement, 21,* 646–666.

Splitter, V., Dobusch, L., von Krogh, G., Whittington, R., & Walgenbach, P. (2023). Openness as organizing principle: Introduction to the special issue. *Organization Studies, 44*(1), 7–27.

Splitter, V., Seidl, D., & Whittington, R. (2019). Practice-theoretical perspectives on open strategy: Implications of a strong programme. In D. Seidl, G. Von Krogh & R. Whittington (Eds.), *Cambridge handbook of open strategy* (pp. 221–240). Cambridge University Press.

Stack, J. (1994). *The great game of business.* Doubleday.

Steger, T., & Hartz, R. (2008). The power of participation? Power relations and processes in employee-owned companies. *German Journal of Human Resource Research, 22*(2), 153.

Stieger, D., Matzler, K., Chatterjee, S., & Ladstaetter-Fussenegger, F. (2012). Democratizing strategy: How crowdsourcing can be used for strategy dialogues. *California Management Review, 54*(4), 44–69.

Stjerne, I., Geraldi, J., & Wenzel, M. (2022). Strategic practice drift: How open strategy infiltrates the strategy process. *Journal of Management Studies,* in print.

Tackx, K., & Verdin, P. (2014). Can co-creation lead to better strategy? An exploratory research. *Universite Libre de Bruxelles*, Working Papers, 14–027.

Tavakoli, A., Schlagwein, D., & Schoder, D. (2015). Open strategy: Consolidated definition and processual conceptualization. In *International conference on information systems(ICIS) 2015*, FortWorth, TX.

Tezel, A., Koskela, L., & Tzortzopoulos, P. (2016). Visual management in production management: A literature synthesis. *Journal of Manufacturing Technology Management, 27*(6), 766–799.

Tortorella, G. L., Cauchick-Miguel, P. A., & Gaiardelli, P. (2018). Hoshin Kanri and A3: A proposal for integrating variability into the policy deployment process. *The TQM Journal, 31*(2), 118–135.

Vaara, E., Rantakari, A., & Holstein, J. (2019). Participation research and open strategy. In D. Seidl, G. von Krogh & R. Whittington (Eds.), *Cambridge handbook of open strategy* (pp. 27–40). Cambridge University Press.

Vaara, E., & Whittington, R. (2012). Strategy-as-practice: Taking social practices seriously. *The Academy of Management Annals, 6*, 285–336.

Von Hippel, E. (2005). *Democratizing innovation*. The MIT Press.

Von Hippel, E., & von Krogh, G. (2016). Identifying viable "need-solution pairs": Problem solving without problem formulation. *Organization Science, 27*(1), 207–221.

Wawarta, C., & Paroutis, S. (2019). Strategy tools in open strategizing: Blessing or curse for making strategy more actionable? In *Academy of Management Science Proceedings, 1*.

Weiser, A. K., Jarzabkowski, P., & Laamanen, T. (2020). Completing the adaptive turn: An integrative view of strategy implementation. *Academy of Management Annals, 14*(2), 969–1031.

West, J., & Gallagher, S. (2006). Challenges of open innovation: The paradox of firm investment in open-source software. *R&D Management, 36*(3), 319–331.

Whitehurst, J. (2015). *The open organization: Igniting passion and performance*. Harvard Business School Press Books.

Whittington, R. (2006). Completing the practice turn in strategy research. *Organization Studies, 27*, 613–634.

Whittington, R. (2019). *Opening strategy: Professional strategists and practice change, 1960 to today*. Oxford University Press.

Whittington, R., Cailluet, L., & Yakis-Douglas, B. (2011). Opening strategy: Evolution of a precarious profession. *British Journal of Management, 22*(3), 531–544.

Wulf, A., & Butel, L. (2016). Knowledge sharing and innovative corporate strategies in collaborative relationships: The potential of open strategy in business ecosystems. In L. Shaofeng, B. Delibašić & F. Oderanti (Eds.), *Decision support systems, 2nd international conference* (pp. 165–181). Springer International Publishing.

Xu, X., & Alexy, O. (2019). Strategic openness and open strategy. In D. Seidl, G. Von Krogh & R. Whittington (Eds.), *Cambridge handbook of open strategy* (pp. 59–84). Cambridge University Press.

Yakis-Douglas, B., Angwin, D., Ahn, K., & Meadows, M. (2017). Opening M&A strategy to investors: Predictors and outcomes of transparency during organizational transition. *Long Range Planning, 50*, 411–422.

3   Digital technologies: The paving road ahead towards open strategizing?

3.1   Techno-economic paradigms: Conceptual roots

Technology is embedded in tacit knowledge. Technology, innovations, and technological progress are complex phenomena encompassing various elements, often unquantifiable and thus hard to define. In today's world, the seminal importance of technological progress is widely acknowledged, and bearing in mind the fact that human knowledge and ideas, technological progress, and economy constitute an evolutionary system, in academic and public debate, technology is treated as a fundamental element of development (Rosenberg, 1994). The elements of this system are inherently related and preconditioned; the impact of technology on the economy and/or society at large is neither immediate nor direct. Unique causal loops emerge, and they drive productivity shifts and business network expansion, enhance innovation emergence and innovativeness, and increase the efficiency and effectiveness of running a business. The earlier-presented understanding of technology coincides with the view of Dosi (1982), who suggests that technological change should be seen through the lens of growing production possibilities and the increasing number of produce. However, in the same work, he also emphasises that technology is something much broader as *a set of pieces of knowledge* (Dosi, 1982, p. 151), encompassing both '*practical*' (related to some practical issues) and '*theoretical*' (related to the knowledge that might be applied to solve some problem, but so far has been not) aspects, but also is strictly associated with all kind of know-how, methods, and procedures, but also a physical stock of devices.

In modern research, technology is no longer treated as proposed by Solow (2016), where it was an unexplained residual; next – in an analogous vein, claimed by Nathan Rosenberg writing about the '*black box*'. Technology is considered an endogenous development factor, embodying the cumulated knowledge and massively impacting society and the economy. This strong emphasis regarding close interrelatedness between knowledge and technology conceptually traces back to claims that knowledge is a non-rivalrous good. To a large extent – which primarily refers to various digital solutions offered,

DOI: 10.4324/9781003424772-3

technology is also a non-rivalrous good. Once it is shared and diffused among society members, each individual can use it effectively, which does not happen at the expense of the other individual. In other words, the marginal cost of knowledge sharing and technology is often close to or equal to zero. The latter is especially valid for various digitally based solutions, like access to wireless networks, where multiplying the number of users does not generate additional costs for the network-providing company. The negligible or even zero-marginal costs of technology dissemination and adoption bring on board the emergence of the unique effects of scale and cutting-edge changes. Technological development, through network effects (network externalities), these path-breaking inventions, profoundly transforms the way that societies and economies work, enforcing revolutionary changes. The latter primarily refers to technologies considered as 'pervasive technologies', hence technologies bringing profound reshaping of the 'present state of the art'. That technological pervasiveness means that new technological solutions are thoroughly implemented not only at the individual level but, above all, that technological innovations are effectively implemented at the company level, and a considerable share of processes is subjected to technology. The latter effectively refers to endogenously driven firm innovations and long-run strategy design and implementation, including open-strategizing approaches.

When looking closer at the firm-level and potential interrelatedness between technology (mainly digital technology), propensity, and necessity to creating innovative solutions and strategies implementation, there may arise a question on whether and to what extent digital environment constitutes a solid fundament enhancing open strategizing windows. Needless to say, a digitally shaped environment enforces inclusive solutions, and open strategizing perfectly encapsulates the latter's essence.

The '*social shaping of technology*' (MacKenzie and Wajcman, 1985 and 1999) is the strand in research that emerged in the 1980s combining technological progress, societies and individuals, social acceptance of technology and social attitudes towards the latter. Ostensibly, the '*social shaping of technology*' approach falls under the broad understanding of the role of new technologies, especially in heading towards open strategizing at the firm level. On the one hand, broad implementation and usage of digital technologies pave avenues towards greater inclusiveness and adoption of a participatory approach (Bagnoli & Clark, 2010; Bergold & Thomas, 2012; Étienne, 2013) in problems' solution in companies, but – on the other – it signals changes in both quality and quantity of demand for novel technological solutions. The latter suggests that this is a society that has the power to shape future technological developments being led by specific needs and brings on board a more extensive '*understanding of the relationship between scientific excellence, technological innovation and economic and social well-being*' (Williams & Edge, 1996, p. 1), indicating the existence of the causal loop between society, economy, and technology. The approach embedded in the '*social shaping of technology*' concept hypothesizes that technological development is not purely deterministic, but rather it is not only that technology shapes socioeconomic systems but these systems also shape future technology development trajectories, including the emergence of technological innovations. Following Dickens (2007) and Takac et al. (2011), the idea that technology is socially, economically, and institutionally embedded seems to gain accuracy. Technological development is not just the 'transformers' of society, economy, or business. However, the onset of technological advancements – or even technological waves if a broader time horizon is considered – is an outcome of embedded debates between economic agents. At the macro-level, the '*social shaping of technology*' is enforced by social, economic, and institutional forces (environment) (Molina, 1992; Bijker & Law, 1992; Bijker, 1995; Bijker et al., 2012), suggesting a quite convergent view of how technological progress is not shaped deterministically but rather 'emphatically' (Dicken, 2007). At the micro level, the '*social shaping of technology*' may be perceived as a growing embeddedness of tacit knowledge of individuals operating in the business sector. Accumulated knowledge and skills signal needs for further technological solutions driving, among other things, more inclusive and open strategy formulation. Such interrelatedness between individuals (and thus societies) and technology as such drives a way towards

> ensuring social and economic fundaments for rapid assimilation of newly emerging technologies; but also providing a technology-friendly environment for fast diffusion of new techniques among individuals, and throughout the economy, preconditions benefiting from technological progress, but also . . . maximising, both social and economic effects, which may arise when new technologies arrive is crucial from the long-term perspective.
>
> (Lechman, 2017, s. 35)

Open and inclusive environment – both at macro and micro level, provokes not only technological progress during next periods but ensures growing dynamics of technological novelties diffusion and social propensity to acquire innovations and learning how to use them effectively. These positive effects of interactions between society (individuals) and technology are even boosted as the positive network externalities arise (Katz & Shapiro, 1985, 1992; Economides, 1996), as these broadly recognized effects are substantive in digital technologies. Societies assess and assimilate technological novelties relying upon 'intellectual' capital (Soete & Verspagen, 1993), societies' readiness and adaptability. However, this is strongly preconditioned by the emerging benefits observable for those joining the network. Digital technologies provide a unique environment for the network effects, strengthening inclusiveness, openness and usage of technological novelties.

Freeman and Pérez (1988) distinguish between four types of technological change. The first type is incremental innovations, which refers to small-scale and progressive modifications of existing products and/or services. Next, the second type is path-breaking radical innovations that profoundly and often abruptly transform already-existing products and processes. The third type of technological change delineated by Freeman and Pérez (1988) is innovations that change the structure of economies, often leading to the emergence of new sectors/branches. Last – the most overwhelming type of technological change – is the one that brings a new techno-economic paradigm, encompassing highly revolutionary changes both on the ground of technology itself and the entire economic system.

3.2   On paradigms

For more than 200 years, they witnessed consecutive technological path-breaking revolutions. Starting from the massive onset of technological change in England during the second part of the eighteenth century, economies and societies underwent four successive technological waves. The last technological revolution, the Fifth Technological Revolution wave, emerged with introducing the microprocessor to the public in 1971, the first personal computer in 1973 (by Intel), and mobile telephony by Motorola during the same year. Historically, these technological waves repeat every 50–70 years and are intimately related to radical social, economic, and institutional shifts. These shifts are labelled as techno-economic paradigms (regimes). The conceptual roots of the techno-economic paradigm trace back to the influential works of Pérez (1986); however, afterwards, this concept was adjusted and augmented by Freeman and Pérez (1986, 1988) and Pérez (2002, 2003, 2009). Conceptually, the techno-economic paradigms rely on Kuhn's (1962) idea to explain shifts in the theoretical perspectives. Dosi (1982) and Dosi et al. (1988) propose the definition of the techno-economic paradigm by putting it into a broad historical context, and they state that 'within' the techno-economic paradigm, there is space created for technological innovations to emerge. Moreover, in Dosi (1982), we find arguments that the concept of techno-economic regimes may be a valuable tool for researching the role of technological progress in production sectors.

In the works of Freeman and Soete (1997) and Pérez (1986), we find arguments that each technological revolution induces its own techno-economic paradigm (regime). Moreover, Pérez (1986) suggests that this newly constituted techno-economic paradigm may be technically perceived as a new technological frontier, encompassing best practices incorporating technological progress. This new frontier is also perceived as an institutional 'frontier' embedding a whole stock of necessary organizational transformation, shifting capital and labour productivity. In Freeman and Pérez (1986, 1988), the definition of techno-economic paradigms is a set of technical and economic features of emerging technological solutions being gradually incorporated into economic systems. The definition proposed by Freeman and Pérez (1988), by convention, imposes that technological progress gradually becomes an integral part of the socioeconomic system. Hence, it enforces radical changes within it. In the same work of Freeman and Pérez (1988), we note a proposition of labelling the techno-economic paradigm as a kind of 'technological revolution' driving the emergence of radical and incremental innovations. Hanna (2010) claims that '*a techno-economic paradigm articulates the technical and organisational model for taking the best advantage of the technological revolution and results in the rejuvenation of the whole productive structure*' (Hanna, 2010, p. 31).

From a company's perspective that pursues the implementation of open strategies, the techno-economic paradigm constitutes conceptual foundations for understanding why technological progress is an essential element of running a business. Relying on the fact that techno-economic regimes enforce the emergence of the integral systems within society and economy, analogous mechanisms are observable on the firm level, creating a unique type of interconnectedness as *a 'technology system'* (see Freeman (1982, 1992) and in Freeman and Soete (1997)). These newly emerged '*technology systems*' demonstrate a strong and long-run impact on the ways of doing business, shaping the business environment and conditions. In this vein, these two essential elements – transparency and inclusiveness – closely related to open strategies gain importance. Notably, both transparency and inclusiveness precondition effective implementation of technological innovation in business processes, production of goods and services, distribution and/or promotion activities. However, what is even more significant in this case is that the within-company processes are driven more effectively if transparency and inclusiveness are induced by technological progress and vice versa. Novel technological solutions – and what especially accounts for digital technologies, not only by their nature of being 'inclusive technologies' (Goggin & Newell, 2007; Beliz et al., 2019) – offer inclusion of knowledge, new ideas into a company's environment making it a more collaborative sphere, providing broader empowerment and agency for a firm's employees. What is worth emphasizing here is that digital technologies, since they create quickly expanding networks, enhance the inclusiveness *per se*. When it comes to transparency, not only do digital technologies enable the 'hyper-transparency' (Mueller, 2015; Rodríguez-Hoyos et al., 2018) over societies and economies but, at the firm level, it leverages effectiveness by easing the flow of knowledge, information *et alia*, and ensuring timely delivery of the latter. What matters most is undeniably the information, knowledge, and ideas-related transparency, which makes the open strategies approach more effective and efficient.

3.3 Digital technologies diffusion

Digital technologies as 'products' of the Fifth Technological Wave are unique for several reasons. Not only do they differ massively from all technologies generated during past technological revolutions but they are the technological tools that never before have been so widely and extensively adopted and used. Digital technologies are cheap to use and can be adopted at nearly zero marginal cost. Digital technologies are easily acquired by low-income and low-educated societies (even illiterate people). Digital technologies are fast and easily installable in remote and geographically isolated regions, in regions severely underdeveloped concerning complex infrastructure. All these make digital technologies rapidly diffusible among social and economic agents.

Indeed, diffusion is driven by different endogenous and exogenous factors. Among the most critical exogenous determinants, we can list elements like price policies, telecommunication market competition type, institutional frameworks, population density, and agents' propensity to buy technological innovations or take risks. Still, as raised in several studies (see, for instance, Lechman, 2016 and 2017), the process of digital technology diffusion is strongly endogenous and hence self-perpetuating. The endogeneity of the process of digital technology diffusion is subjected to the unique network effects (network externalities) that emerge during the early stages of diffusion.

The issue of network effects was raised and, to some point, clarified in the works of Katz and Shapiro (1985), Chou and Shy (1990), Shapiro and Varian (1998), and Clements (2004), who underlined that the economic and social effects of the implementation of the technological advancements they predominantly rely on the number of new users, the extent to which individuals acquire and use newly emerging technological solutions. The network effects emerge once the number of individuals wishing to pay and acquire new technology grows substantially, and the latter effectively drive further increases in technology saturation levels. In Loch and Huberman (1999), we trace claims that positive network effects arise even under the uncertainty that is inherent in technology diffusion systems, but the point is that economic agents tend to imitate the behaviour of others; they repeat the choices of early innovators and early adopters. In that sense, it is arguably reasonable to state that the network effects unveil societal tendencies to imitate, which, in effect, constitutes the diffusion itself. To a large extent, this positive feedback from early constituted networks arises when the density of interpersonal communication is substantive. Hence, various communication channels work effectively, and people share knowledge regarding the benefits of adopting technological innovations.

Interestingly, the central point is that network externalities are intimately related to the process of technology diffusion, and – by definition – they emerge as positive feedback from random contacts among economic agents, and that drives the rapid growth of the network itself (Valente, 1996 and 2023; Lechman, 2016). According to Markus (1987), the network effects are positive re-alimentation schema that enforces sustainable multiplication of new users of introduced technological innovations, rapidly leading to exponential growth of new users. These claims of Markus (1987) coincide with the empirical evidence on the technology diffusion process, demonstrating that it follows the sigmoid patterns with its exponential growth phase.

The process of technology diffusion can be easily described by the sigmoid (S-shaped, logistic) curve, along which three characteristic phases are easily detectable. During the first (initial) stage of diffusion, the process proceeds at a slow – sometimes even spasmodic – rate; it is easily reversible and takes a long time to increase the saturation levels. However, as more and more agents notice the benefits offered by new technologies and regard joining the network as beneficial, they acquire new technologies and start using them. Formally, joining the network often occurs even in the state of non-dropping or even increasing prices; however, the potential future benefits that economic agents expect to achieve when using new technological solutions exceed their current costs. When individuals massively adopt new technologies, this particular effect is labelled network effects (network externalities) and constitutes one of the prime factors driving technology diffusion. The emergence of these network externalities and achievement of the critical mass (see, for example, in Marwell & Oliver, 1993; Economides & Himmelberg, 2013; Lechman, 2016) allows leaving the early diffusion stage, heading toward technological takeoff (Kuznets, 1963; Berrill, 1964; Rostow, 1972; Lechman, 2016) and entering the second phase along sigmoid diffusion curve. During the second diffusion stage, the technology is adopted at an exponential rate, and hence, the society, economy, and markets are fast heading towards full saturation. Once the diffusion process slows down – usually as markets are close to full saturation or unexpected exogenous factors impede the process – we enter the third phase, during which no rapid changes in the level of new technology adoption are reported.

Available empirical evidence unequivocally supports the supposition that digital technologies diffuse historically unprecedentedly due to network externalities. Such claims may be traced in the works of Lechman (2016 and 2017), Das et al. (2018), Kallal et al. (2021) or Saba and Ngepah (2022); additionally, a significant stock of evidence shows that digital technologies diffusion is subjected to the emergence network effects demonstrating strong endogeneity of the process (see, for instance, works of Baliamoune-Lutz, 2003; Grazzi & Jung, 2019; Elstner et al., 2022). Statistical data from the International Telecommunication Union unequivocally support our claim on the rapid expansion of digital technologies worldwide. Figure 3.1 exemplifies this global expansion of digital technologies. The picture later approximates developed diffusion curves for three fundamental macro ICT indicators: mobile cellular telephony penetration rates (per 100 inhabitants); active mobile broadband penetration rates (per 100 inhabitants); and internet users (as a share of total population).

Considering basic statistical facts regarding ICT's growing adoption and usage globally, we note massive shifts between 2005 and 2023. The world average penetration rates increased from 33.9% to 110.6%, 4% to 87.4%, and 15.6% to 67.4% for MCS, AMS, and IU accordingly. As for the data on mobile telephony usage in 2023, on average, the saturation

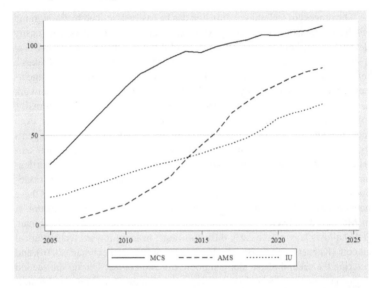

Figure 3.1 Digital technologies global diffusion trajectories. Averaged world data. Period 2005–2023.

Source: Authors' elaboration. Note: on Y-axis – saturation rates; MCS – mobile cellular subscriptions; AMS – active mobile broadband subscriptions; IU – internet users; logistic growth model (Meyer, 1994; Tsoularis & Wallace, 2002; Kucharavy & De Guio, 2015) applied to estimate the curves.

rate exceeded 100%, suggesting full world coverage with this technology, and we desegregate this data by geographic region.[1] Only in Africa is the coverage below 100% (92.3% according to ITU statistics). These primary data clearly show how fast digital technologies diffuse worldwide, supporting – to a large extent – our claims on the uniqueness of these technologies themselves and the historically unprecedented rate of diffusion of technological innovations.

These numbers, however, not only demonstrate that – in fact, all society members and economic agents rapidly gained access to digital technologies and were able to use them for different purposes, but also, the Fifth Digital Revolution created a kind of new digital reality enforcing transformation of mindsets, attitudes, ways of communication, and modes of doing business. The inside company-enforced changes are as massive as those in the external environment, and these two realities are interdependent and create a specific causal loop. The digital transformation and digitally driven adjustments are observable inside individual companies (Matt et al., 2015; Gobble, 2018; Van Alstyne & Parker, 2021; Holopainen et al., 2023), and unquestionably they constitute a significant driver of, for instance, approaches to strategies formulation and execution, but also they may re-define roles that company employees play. This employee role redefinition (see, for example, Kong et al., 2023) can potentially combine greater involvement in strategy formulation or decision-making processes. Digital technologies carry the potential to implement the participatory approach in company's management to effectively engage people's skills, innovative ideas, and knowledge (tacit and non-tacit), facilitate the flow of information, and eradicate information asymmetries, which, in the longer time horizon, brings opportunities for shifts in gaining competitive advantage.

3.4 Towards ICT-enabled open strategizing. Unlocking the potential of open strategies

Digital technologies such as General Purpose Technologies (GPTs hereafter) (Helpman, 1998; Jovanovic & Rousseau, 2005; Bresnahan, 2010) provide numerous technological innovations and penetrate all social, institutional, economic, and business spheres. Digital technologies once proliferate rapidly in entire societies and economies; they also overwhelm the environment at the firm level, reshaping the companies' function (Ardolino et al., 2018; Martinez-Caro et al., 2020; Ancillai et al., 2023). As augmented earlier, digital technologies demonstrate the enormous ability to spread rapidly and unique features, generating novel and innovative environments for macro-scale operations but also those at the micro level (firm level). However, let us take a look at these elements from a different perspective. Digital technologies are factors that enforce certain behaviours, ways of communication and knowledge sharing, ways of doing business, ways of shaping state and entrepreneurship development policies, or strategies design. Notably, these changes enforced and opportunities offered by digital technologies are detectable – although not easily definable or quantifiable, especially at the company level.

Enterprises are usually prone to elements that an economy is composed of (e.g. institutions, government policies, and legal frameworks) and are highly exposed to both the positive and negative influences of technological changes. The business sector is not digitally neutral; it is affected in multiple ways. This digital dependency is exhibited in the IT-related sector and proliferates in all business types. This digital proliferation of the business sector paves new avenues towards developing new products and services and new markets gaining or shaping consumers' behaviours. From the inside company perspective, digital technologies facilitate certain types of implemented business models and strategy building.

Digital technologies and the disruptive digital environment that these technologies enhance, on the other hand, enforce the emergence of new business models, ensuring harmonious co-existence. These new technological innovations and business models lead to profit maximization, gaining a dominant position in the market, etc. (Guo et al., 2019). The latter involves drawing insights into considering in the business running ICT-based new dynamic capabilities, skills upgrading and, for instance, adopting new approaches to the firm's hierarchy understanding (including the decision-making process), steps to eradicate information asymmetries and thus facilitate unrestricted flows of ideas, knowledge, and information itself. This novel approach to business model perception unquestionably strengthens the positive impact of digital technologies on the business environment and businesses themselves. The fitting of digital technologies and business evolves, enhancing company processes to transform in a way that maximizes benefits and sustains competitive advantages that ICT offers (Koch & Windsperger, 2017). Afterwards, the transformation within company processes shall bring strategic advantages and open market opportunities (Oliver, 2018). The digital environment also seems to offer unique opportunities for business alliances (Dyer & Singh, 1998) – business ecosystems and their explosion due to enormously growing ways of communication, value creation, information, and knowledge sharing. As defined by Koch and Windsperger (2017), followed by Selander et al. (2013, pp. 184): '*a digital business ecosystem can be understood as "a collective" of firms that are inter-linked by a common interest in the prosperity of a digital technology for materialising their own product or service innovation*'. In the following steps, these business alliances lead to multi-firm networks, allowing for even more significant expansion and exploitation of opportunities offered by digital technologies. In this vein, the network theory (Borgatti & Foster, 2003; Snow & Fjeldstad, 2015) offers an even more profound understanding of the role of digital technologies in the business environment and businesses themselves since it shifts the focus from the single economic agent to their interdependency and relations. Granovetter's theory (Granovetter, 1979 and 2017; Tutić & Wiese, 2015) of the strength of weak ties even adds to this logic and sequence of events since it claims that strengthening networks makes the weaker ties work more effectively and thus facilitates, for example, the diffusion of information and knowledge. Significantly, according to Granovetter's theory, the inter-network ties usually emerge randomly, following unstructured trajectories, which brings a potential of structural hole elimination (Zaheer & Bell, 2005; Burt, 2015 and 2018), making the organizations work more effectively. Considering the inter-organizational networks as the source of resources and capabilities (Uzzi, 1996), these ties notably alter business efficiency and effectiveness, making the digital environment and digital business models more and more reliant.

Taking a more global look at the business models operating in the digital environment, there comes to mind another concept of a network-centric (Chandra & Wilkinson, 2017; Srinivasan & Venkatraman, 2018) business model that relies on inter-organizational network structure. Such network-centric business models usually emerge under dynamic digital ecosystems, in which the transformative logic of strategy-making is mostly adopted and creates values using firms' values in co-creating. Conceptually, digital business models are inherently related to various networks, and, as clarified in previous sections, digital technologies are technological innovations that drive the rise of these networks. Such perception of these opens up a new perspective in the business itself, not only from the perspective of its economic activity or, for example, values creation but foremost from the perspective of it within the company's social and human capital and – already mentioned – open strategies to be built.

Digital technologies, as path-breaking and General Purpose Technologies, have a unique ability to create new networks. The networks developed due to digital technologies not only account for business networks, global value chains, networks of stock exchanges, or communication networks but these technologies enhance different types of social networks. These social networks facilitate interpersonal communication and the flow of ideas, knowledge, and innovative thoughts; they enable the eradication of information asymmetries – one of the major market failures causing decreases in economic efficiency. Social networks work effectively as they rely on transparency, openness, and inclusiveness, and all these three listed elements may be claimed as core fundaments of the open strategy approach being pursued in a growing number of companies.

Notably, a company's open strategy approach to strategy building seems to be significantly positively influenced by the digital environment. This novel paradigm in approaches to companies formulation (Matzler et al., 2014; Adobor, 2021) is not only perceived as an innovation-generating concept (Pittz & Adler, 2023) or allowing to attain competitive advantage (Mohammadian & Bafti, 2023) but it involves inclusive approaches, transparency, and creativity to be widely implemented. The inside company perspective allows perceiving digital technologies as a factor facilitating the implementation of an open strategy approach. In Morton et al. (2020), we find various claims that digital technologies reshape the nature of work in strategies and the work of strategists. To some point, the open strategy can be labelled as a digitally enabled practice. Morton et al. (2020), the authors point out that '*IT-enabled openness in strategy has received significant interest recently; few studies have focused on the specific (digital) work practices of strategists and subsequently connected this to notable outcomes such as organisational transformation*'. They develop four conceptual models to answer the seminal question on the interrelatedness of digitalization, work organization, management, adoption of open strategy approach, and thus the organisation's transformation. Whittington (2014), in an analogous vein, emphasized that technology plays a central role in open strategy building since it allows for deeper involvement of all stakeholders in strategy building. Seidl et al. (2019) also emphasize that, on the one hand, the role of digital technologies in enhancing open strategy is pivotal since it allows for more excellent information flow, and thus transparency et alia, but – on the other – open strategy is a concept embraces transparency and inclusiveness themselves. Henceforth, the specific causal loop emergence shows that digital technologies and open strategy simultaneously enable and enhance their existence. In even earlier work of Jarzabkowski and Wolf (2010), we trace a clear statement that the type of technology – in our case, digital technology – provides insights into interpersonal communications, promoting greater inclusiveness and hence the role of employees in strategy building. Due to the use of digital tools, the company's community can actively communicate, discuss, and express their ideas and concerns; all these – and more – bring the potential to generate strategic content towards reshaped emergent strategy when all stakeholders are involved. Needless to say, top managers' understanding of the strategic input from the community is a prerequisite to benefit fully from the open strategy approach implemented. When top managers genuinely wish to realize and benefit from the open strategy concept, they are responsive, promote advocacy campaigns, and shape their priorities according to the community's needs and concerns. A radical change towards the organization membership model is on the way. The ensured trans-community transparency, visibility, and consistency effectuate the 'strategizing together' process, shifting the organization towards an openness-based organization with inclusive and transparent strategizing realized. Thanks to the adoption of digital technology and the reshaping of entrepreneurial and managerial mindsets, the strategy-building process no longer remains in the hands of the 'company's elite' (Chandler, 1962).

However, instead, this process is distributed across members of the organization. Including broader actors in strategy building and, thus, developing open strategy may be enhanced by analogue and digital means (Hautz et al., 2017). However, using analogue means, the group of stakeholders included is usually limited. In contrast, being digitally based means facilitating entire inclusion, leaving room for the individual to decide if they wish to participate in strategy building. Individual stakeholders' contribution to open strategy building is somewhat limited by their skills, knowledge, and/or bounded rationality. Still, the widespread use of digital technologies may partially eliminate these drawbacks, especially by contributing to skill upgrading and eradicating information asymmetries. The company's stakeholders' involvement in the strategy-building process works two-directionally. First, in the short-term perspective, the company can head towards benefits maximization through employees' broader participation – primarily by improving their strategic decisions, and second – the inclusion of employees ensures their long-term engagement in the firm's processes (Plotnikova et al., 2021).

In a broader sense, open strategizing involves including the firm's customers and acknowledging their role in company marketing and production strategy building. Nonetheless, again, digital technologies are perfectly enabling this process. Co-creation and deeper integration of customers in product future designing massively facilitated mass communication tools, customization techniques, and customer segmentation. Even though this learning from customers does not necessarily directly imply their close involvement in the firm's strategy designing, co-strategizing with customers is more 'distant' than close stakeholders, but still, it leaves much room to decide which experiences and signals from customers are used in an open strategy. Digital technology shapes long-term interaction within and outside companies and transforms short-run activities. The social shaping of technology concept argues, however, that people also drive changes in technological progress. In the case of relations like open strategy and digital technology, this is even more obvious since the stakeholders' and firm's customers' needs and actions signal future changes in technological development.

To sum up, elements like openness, inclusiveness, and transparency stand at the core of the open strategy approach. Open strategy as an inclusive strategy relies on the broad participation of the company's stakeholders and benefits from their knowledge, skills, and ideas-sharing, bringing novel approaches and benefits maximization on board. Technologies as such demonstrate the enormous potential to be helpful in strategy design. However, these digital solutions enhance greater transparency, information, ideas, and knowledge sharing among the company's employees. This participatory approach facilitated by digital technologies lies at the centre of the open strategizing concept. Many claim that digital technologies are drivers for the participatory approach pursued in companies and should be perceived as an enabling factor, a prerequisite to implementing open strategies. This is mainly because digital technologies create various networks, a perfect transmission channel between top managers, 'regular' employees, and customers. The digital environment seems to set a perfect ground for open strategies; the match seems ideal, and even more, it works two-directionally.

The perfect interplay between digital technologies and open strategies, in effect, fosters innovativeness, local and global innovability, knowledge sharing, and global partnership development. This synergy drives business advantages, competitive advantage, and growing market shares and position.

Note

1 See www.itu.int/en/ITU-D/Statistics/Pages/stat/default.aspx (accessed: 20th Dec 2023).

References

Adobor, H. (2021). Open strategy: What is the impact of national culture? *Management Research Review, 44*(9), 1277–1297.

Ancillai, C., Sabatini, A., Gatti, M., & Perna, A. (2023). Digital technology and business model innovation: A systematic literature review and future research agenda. *Technological Forecasting and Social Change, 188*, 122307.

Ardolino, M., Rapaccini, M., Saccani, N., Gaiardelli, P., Crespi, G., & Ruggeri, C. (2018). The role of digital technologies for the service transformation of industrial companies. *International Journal of Production Research, 56*(6), 2116–2132.

Bagnoli, A., & Clark, A. (2010). Focus groups with young people: A participatory approach to research planning. *Journal of Youth studies, 13*(1), 101–119.

Baliamoune-Lutz, M. (2003). An analysis of the determinants and effects of ICT diffusion in developing countries. *Information Technology for Development, 10*(3), 151–169.

Beliz, G., Basco, A. I., & de Azevedo, B. (2019). Harnessing the opportunities of inclusive technologies in a global economy. *Economics, 13*(1), 20190006.

Bergold, J., & Thomas, S. (2012). Participatory research methods: A methodological approach in motion. *Historical Social Research/Historische Sozialforschung*, 191–222.

Berrill, K. (1964). Historical experience: The problem of economic "Take-Off". In *Economic development with special reference to East Asia: Proceedings of a conference held by the international economic association* (pp. 233–251). Palgrave Macmillan UK.

Bijker, W. (1995). Sociohistorical technology studies. In S. Jasanoff, G. Markle, J. Peterson & T. Pinch (Eds.), *Handbook of science and technology studies*. The MIT Press.

Bijker, W. E., Hughes, T. P., Pinch, T., & Douglas, D. G. (2012). *The social construction of technological systems: New directions in the sociology and history of technology*. MIT Press.

Bijker, W. E., & Law, J. (1992). *Shaping technology/building society: Studies in sociotechnical change*. MIT Press.

Borgatti, S. P., & Foster, P. C. (2003). The network paradigm in organizational research: A review and typology. *Journal of Management, 29*(6), 991–1013.

Bresnahan, T. (2010). General purpose technologies. *Handbook of the Economics of Innovation, 2*, 761–791.

Burt, R. S. (2015). Reinforced structural holes. *Social Networks, 43*, 149–161.

Burt, R. S. (2018). Structural holes. In *Social stratification* (pp. 659–663). Routledge.

Chandler, A. D. (1962). *Strategy and structure: Chapters in the history of American industrial enterprises*. MIT Press.

Chandra, Y., & Wilkinson, I. F. (2017). Firm internationalization from a network-centric complex-systems perspective. *Journal of World Business, 52*(5), 691–701.

Chou, C. F., & Shy, O. (1990). Network effects without network externalities. *International Journal of Industrial Organization, 8*(2), 259–270.

Clements, M. T. (2004). Direct and indirect network effects: Are they equivalent? *International Journal of Industrial Organization, 22*(5), 633–645.

Das, A., Chowdhury, M., & Seaborn, S. (2018). ICT diffusion, financial development and economic growth: New evidence from low and lower middle-income countries. *Journal of the Knowledge Economy, 9*, 928–947.

Dicken, P. (2007). *Global shift: Mapping the changing contours of the world economy*. Sage Publications

Dosi, G. (1982). Technological paradigms and technological trajectories: A suggested interpretation of the determinants and directions of technical change. *Research Policy, 11*(3), 147–162.

Dosi G., Freeman, C., Nelson, R. & Soete, L. (Eds.). (1988). *Technical change and economic theory*. Columbia University Press

Dyer, J. H., & Singh, H. (1998). The relational view: Cooperative strategy and sources of interorganizational competitive advantage. *Academy of Management Review, 23*(4), 660–679.

Economides, N. (1996). Network externalities, complementarities, and invitations to enter. *European Journal of Political Economy, 12*(2), 211–233.

Economides, N., & Himmelberg, C. (2013). Critical mass and network evolution in telecommunications. In *Toward a competitive telecommunication industry* (pp. 47–63). Routledge.

Elstner, S., Grimme, C., Kecht, V., & Lehmann, R. (2022). The diffusion of technological progress in ICT. *European Economic Review, 149*, 104277.

Étienne, M. (Ed.). (2013). *Companion modelling: A participatory approach to support sustainable development*. Springer Science & Business Media.

Freeman, C. (1982). *The economics of industrial innovation*. MIT, Cambridge.

Freeman, C. (1992). *The economics of hope: Essays on technical change and economic growth*. Pinter.

Freeman, C., & Pérez, C. (1986). *The diffusion of technical innovations and changes of techno-economic paradigm*. Science Policy Research Unit University of Sussex.

Freeman, C., & Pérez, C. (1988). *Structural crises of adjustment, business cycles and investment behaviour*. Pinter.

Freeman, C., & Soete, L. (1997). *The economics of industrial innovation*. Pinter.

Gobble, M. M. (2018). Digital strategy and digital transformation. *Research-Technology Management, 61*(5), 66–71.

Goggin, G., & Newell, C. (2007). The business of digital disability. *The Information Society, 23*(3), 159–168.

Granovetter, M. (1979). The idea of "advancement" in theories of social evolution and development. *American Journal of Sociology, 85*(3), 489–515.

Granovetter, M. (2017). *Society and economy: Framework and principles.* Harvard University Press.

Grazzi, M., & Jung, J. (2019). What are the drivers of ICT diffusion? Evidence from Latin American firms. *Information Technologies & International Development, 15*, 15.

Guo, H., Yang, J., & Han, J. (2019). The fit between value proposition innovation and technological innovation in the digital environment: Implications for the performance of startups. *IEEE Transactions on Engineering Management, 68*(3), 797–809.

Hanna, N. K. (2010). *Transforming government and building the information society: Challenges and opportunities for the developing world.* Springer.

Hautz, J., Seidl, D., & Whittington, R. (2017). Open strategy: Dimensions, dilemmas, dynamics. *Long Range Planning, 50*(3), 298–309.

Helpman, E. (Ed.). (1998). *General purpose technologies and economic growth.* MIT Press.

Holopainen, M., Saunila, M., & Ukko, J. (2023). Value creation paths of organizations undergoing digital transformation. *Knowledge and Process Management, 30*(2), 125–136.

Jarzabkowski, P., & Wolf, C. (2010). An activity-theory approach to strategy as practice. *Cambridge handbook of strategy as practice* (pp. 127–140). Cambridge University Press.

Jovanovic, B., & Rousseau, P. L. (2005). General purpose technologies. In *Handbook of economic growth* (Vol. 1. pp. 1181–1224). Elsevier.

Kallal, R., Haddaji, A., & Ftiti, Z. (2021). ICT diffusion and economic growth: Evidence from the sectorial analysis of a periphery country. *Technological Forecasting and Social Change, 162*, 120403.

Katz, M. L., & Shapiro, C. (1985). Network externalities, competition, and compatibility. *The American Economic Review, 75*(3), 424–440.

Katz, M. L., & Shapiro, C. (1992). Product introduction with network externalities. *The Journal of Industrial Economics*, 55–83.

Koch, T., & Windsperger, J. (2017). Seeing through the network: Competitive advantage in the digital economy. *Journal of Organization Design, 6*, 1–30.

Kong, G., Huang, J., & Liu, S. (2023). Digital transformation and within-firm pay gap: Evidence from China. *Emerging Markets Finance and Trade, 59*(6), 1748–1766.

Kucharavy, D., & De Guio, R. (2015). Application of logistic growth curve. *Procedia Engineering, 131*, 280–290.

Kuhn, T. (1962). *The structure of scientific revolutions.* University of Chicago Press.

Kuznets, S. (1963). Notes on the take-off. In *The economics of take-off into sustained growth: Proceedings of a conference held by the international economic association* (pp. 22–43). Palgrave Macmillan.

Lechman, E. (2016). *ICT diffusion in developing countries.* Springer International Publishing.

Lechman, E. (2017). *The diffusion of information and communication technologies*. Routledge.

Loch, C. H., & Huberman, B. A. (1999). A punctuated-equilibrium model of technology diffusion. *Management Science, 45*(2), 160–177.

MacKenzie, D., & Wajcman, J. (1999). *The social shaping of technology*. Open University Press.

Markus, M. L. (1987). Toward a "critical mass" theory of interactive media: Universal access, interdependence and diffusion. *Communication Research, 14*(5), 491–511.

Martínez-Caro, E., Cegarra-Navarro, J. G., & Alfonso-Ruiz, F. J. (2020). Digital technologies and firm performance: The role of digital organisational culture. *Technological Forecasting and Social Change, 154*, 119962.

Marwell, G., & Oliver, P. (1993). *The critical mass in collective action*. Cambridge University Press.

Matt, C., Hess, T., & Benlian, A. (2015). Digital transformation strategies. *Business & Information Systems Engineering, 57*, 339–343.

Matzler, K., Füller, J., Koch, B., Hautz, J., & Hutter, K. (2014). Open strategy – a new strategy paradigm? *Strategie Und Leadership: Festschrift Für Hans H. Hinterhuber*, 37–55.

Meyer, P. (1994). Bi-logistic growth. *Technological Forecasting and Social Change, 47*(1), 89–102.

Mohammadian, B., & Bafti, A. S. (2023). Open strategy and competitive advantage in the age of digital transformation. In *Transformation for sustainable business and management practices: Exploring the spectrum of industry 5.0* (pp. 31–40). Emerald Publishing Limited.

Molina, A. H. (1992). *The social basis of the microelectronics revolution*. Edinburgh University Press.

Morton, J., Wilson, A. D., & Cooke, L. (2020). The digital work of strategists: Using open strategy for organizational transformation. *The Journal of Strategic Information Systems, 29*(2), 101613.

Mueller, M. L. (2015). Hyper-transparency and social control: Social media as magnets for regulation. *Telecommunications Policy, 39*(9), 804–810.

Oliver, J. J. (2018). Strategic transformations in a disruptive digital environment. *Strategic Direction, 34*(5), 5–8.

Pérez, C. (1986). Las nuevas tecnologías: Una visión de conjunto. *Estudios Internacionales*, 420–459.

Pérez, C. (2002). *Technological revolutions and financial capital: The dynamics of bubbles and golden ages*. Edward Elgar Publishing.

Pérez, C. (2003). Technological change and opportunities for development as a moving target. In *Trade and development: Directions for the 21st century* (p. 100). Edward Elgar Publishing.

Pérez, C. (2009). Technological revolutions and techno-economic paradigms. *Cambridge Journal of Economics, 34*(1), 185–202.

Pittz, T. G., & Adler, T. R. (2023). Open strategy as a catalyst for innovation: Evidence from cross-sector social partnerships. *Journal of Business Research, 160*, 113696.

Plotnikova, A., Pandza, K., & Sales-Cavalcante, H. (2021). How strategy professionals develop and sustain an online strategy community – The lessons from Ericsson. *Long Range Planning, 54*(5), 102015.

Rodríguez-Hoyos, A., Estrada-Jiménez, J., Urquiza-Aguiar, L., Parra-Arnau, J., & Forné, J. (2018, April). Digital hyper-transparency: Leading e-government against privacy. In *2018 international conference on eDemocracy & eGovernment (ICEDEG)* (pp. 263–268). IEEE.

Rosenberg, N. (1994). *Exploring the black box: Technology, economics, and history.* Cambridge University Press.

Rostow, W. W. (1972). *The diffusion of power* (Vol. 10). Macmillan.

Saba, C. S., & Ngepah, N. (2022). ICT diffusion, industrialisation and economic growth nexus: An international cross-country analysis. *Journal of the Knowledge Economy, 13*(3), 2030–2069.

Seidl, D., von Krogh, G., & Whittington, R. (2019). *Cambridge handbook of open strategy.* Cambridge University Press.

Selander, L., Henfridsson, O., & Svahn, F. (2013). Capability search and redeem across digital ecosystems. *Journal of Information Technology, 28*, 183–197.

Shapiro, C., & Varian, H. R. (1998). Network effects. In *Notes to accompany information rules: A strategic guide to the network economy.* Harvard Business School Press.

Snow, C. C., & Fjeldstad, O. D. (2015). Network paradigm: Applications in organizational science. In M. Wright (Ed.), *International encyclopedia of the social & behavioral sciences* (Vol. 16, 2nd ed., pp. 546–550). Oxford: Elsevier.

Soete, L., & Verspagen, B. (1993). Technology and growth: The complex dynamics of catching-up, falling behind and taking over. In A. Szirmai (Ed.), *Explaining economic growth.* Elsevier.

Solow, R. M. (2016). Resources and economic growth. *The American Economist, 61*(1), 52–60.

Srinivasan, A., & Venkatraman, N. (2018). Entrepreneurship in digital platforms: A network-centric view. *Strategic Entrepreneurship Journal, 12*(1), 54–71.

Takac, C., Hinz, O., & Spann, M. (2011). The social embeddedness of decision making: Opportunities and challenges. *Electronic Markets, 21*, 185–195.

Tsoularis, A., & Wallace, J. (2002). Analysis of logistic growth models. *Mathematical Biosciences, 179*(1), 21–55.

Tutić, A., & Wiese, H. (2015). Reconstructing Granovetter's network theory. *Social Networks, 43*, 136–148.

Uzzi, B. (1996). The sources and consequences of embeddedness for the economic performance of organizations: The network effect. *American Sociological Review*, 674–698.

Valente, T. W. (1996). Social network thresholds in the diffusion of innovations. *Social Networks, 18*(1), 69–89.

Valente, T. W. (2023). Network interventions: Using social networks to accelerate diffusion of innovations. In *The Sage handbook of social network analysis* (p. 282). Sage.

Van Alstyne, M. W., & Parker, G. G. (2021). Digital transformation changes how companies create value. *Harvard Business Review*. December.

Whittington, R. (2014). Information systems strategy and strategy-as-practice: A joint agenda. *The Journal of Strategic Information Systems*, *23*(1), 87–91.

Williams, R., & Edge, D. (1996). The social shaping of technology. *Research Policy*, *25*(6), 865–899.

Zaheer, A., & Bell, G. G. (2005). Benefiting from network position: Firm capabilities, structural holes, and performance. *Strategic Management Journal*, *26*(9), 809–825.

4 Strategic practices in the digital context. Tracing challenges

4.1 Flyer

This chapter concerns the strategy process exploiting mainly the strategy-as-practice approach – one of the central theoretical debates in the strategy area. Digital technology is changing the nature of strategizing. Open strategy is an emerging information technology (IT)-enabled strategizing practice (Whittington et al., 2011). Therefore, there is a need to pay closer attention to the role of digitalization in strategy practices (Prashantham & Healey, 2022). Thus, the primary locus is to present how organizational practice, praxis, and practitioners are driven by digitalization to gain transparency and inclusiveness (as open strategy dimensions). This chapter discusses different organizational, managerial, and individual aspects influencing strategizing in a digital context. For instance, managers tend to use prior experience, favouring strategic choices they are familiar with (Gavetti & Levinthal, 2000) over unfamiliar options that could achieve digital change.

Moreover, the lack of digitalization experience is another significant aspect/ barrier to strategizing practices (El Sawy et al., 2016). Furthermore, usually routinized, strategizing practices link different entities constructing everyday strategy practices through their identities and specific experiences as strategy practitioners. The role of organizational practices in strategizing highlights the importance of structuring and replicating strategy practices. The capability perspective, especially the dynamic capabilities framework explaining how firms respond to rapid technological change (Eisenhardt & Martin, 2000), is also essential to discuss from the perspective of the IT-enabled practice.

Specifying selected organizational, managerial, and individual aspects to conduct strategic organizational practices that have evolved under the influence of ICT shifts show how these drivers affect strategizing practices by explaining their impact on open strategizing with digital enablement.

4.2 Changing nature of strategizing. Strategy-as-practice perspective

In the face of current challenges, strategic management focuses on primary vital interests in strategic processes, practices, and strategy implementation.

DOI: 10.4324/9781003424772-4

In more detail, the attention is directed to the content and process of formulating and implementing the strategy.

However, the focus on the content of the strategy goes towards what the company's strategy should be. It ignores such essential issues as the contextual conditions for the implementation of this strategy and issues related to what managers can do to increase the chance that this strategy will be proposed and accepted by those in the organization who have the best understanding of the market, technological, and competitive reality (Whittington, 2012). One of the advantages of ignoring implementation and processes is that no strategic idea seems too far-fetched or improbable. Unfortunately, in reality, managers do not have this comfort.

Today, it is necessary to consider the human factor much more in the strategy process. Until recently, humans were relatively isolated from most strategic processes, and the anthropomorphized organization was considered an entity that has a will and acts purposefully. Today, access to technology creates a need for significant participation and communication.

In the strategy process, focusing on the processes and practices that constitute the organization's everyday activities and relate to strategic outcomes is essential.

The strategy process seen from the strategy-as-practice perspective means focusing on the activities that constitute the formulation of a strategy. The shift towards practices leads to an increased interest in social practices. The strategy-as-practice approach responds to challenges regarding the organizational dynamics and practices that constitute the internal context of the strategy process. This is reflected primarily in the shift from a static, factual approach to organization to a process approach. The consequence of moving away from this static, reified pattern in the study of practices is to return the actor to processes (Schatzki, 1997).

The strategy-as-practice approach focuses primarily on activities at the micro level (Felin & Foss, 2005), which make up the so-called strategizing in connection with the context, that is, the macro level. Strategizing is understood as a process, a way of thinking and acting strategically.

References to three components are essential for the strategy-as-practice approach: practices (shared routines of behaviour, including traditions, norms, and procedures for thinking, acting, and using 'things'), practitioners (strategy's actors, the strategists who both perform this activity and carry its practices), and praxis (actual activity, what people do in practice) (Whittington, 2006).

These three elements are the basis of strategy processes at the micro level (strategizing) and, at the same time, distinguish existing approaches based on a reified understanding of the company and strategy.

4.3 Strategizing practices in a digital context

Practice theory (Schatzki, 1996) becomes particularly useful in understanding the organization and strategy process (Jarzabkowski et al., 2016; Whittington,

2006). As a unit of analysis, practice is 'a temporally unfolding and spatially dispersed nexus of doings and sayings' (Schatzki, 1996, p. 89). Organizations are as social and physical spaces created through 'shared routines of behaviour, including traditions, norms, and procedures for thinking, acting, and using things' (Whittington, 2006, p. 619). Practices are repeated patterns of behaviour. However, they provide space for improvisations and workarounds while leaving a certain amount of freedom necessary to achieve the expected results (Jarzabkowski et al., 2016, p. 250).

Organizations' practices mean more than human action and require considering the components that constitute the social world, that is, things. To understand and identify practices, it is necessary to simultaneously see how 'bodily, material and discursive resources' are organized (Jarzabkowski et al., 2015, p. S27). If we adopt such a point of view, practices are also shaped by the possibilities and limitations of (digital) technologies (Hansen & Flyverbom, 2015).

Advances in digital technology influence the traditional nature of the strategy process. The use of digital technologies may provide new opportunities. However, organizations can exploit these opportunities with the right mindset for change, appropriate digital routines, and structural changes. What is essential in the entire discourse on digital technologies is that digital transformation is not only about technology. It has created new ways of thinking about the context of strategy and new ways of strategizing.

When it comes to the phases and routines of an open strategy, the following are indicated: idea generation (e.g. Whittington et al., 2011), decision-making (e.g. Pittz & Adler, 2016), strategy communication (e.g. Dobusch & Gegenhuber, 2015), or all of them.

Practices describe the routines, norms, and tools for executing strategies. These are specific, detailed strategizing practices (Whittington, 2006) that ultimately contribute to and constitute the overall practice. Strategic practices, as already mentioned, may already be available within the organization or may be introduced from outside. Regardless, practices concern common, situational, embodied, and materially mediated strategy routines, for example, through digital technologies (Huang et al., 2014; Whittington, 2006). They are shared between practitioners with similar knowledge and emotional states in similar contexts (Reckwitz, 2002; Vaara & Whittington, 2012). They allow practitioners to act collectively (Jarzabkowski et al., 2007). For example, conducting and participating in strategy meetings (strategy meetings held in a dedicated, physically separate location) is such a strategizing practice (Hodgkinson et al., 2006; Whittington, 2007). Practices are social and material in nature (Baptista et al., 2017; Whittington, 2015). For this reason, practices are socio-material (cf. Stein et al., 2014). When initiating practices, practitioners appropriate material artefacts and tools that are inextricably linked to the practice and are perceived as one. For example, IS/IT-specific artefacts (e.g. computers, applications, business intelligence tools), physical artefacts (e.g. whiteboards, flipcharts) and analytical techniques (e.g. SWOT analysis) will be part of the strategizing practices. The same artefacts can be part of different practices, serve different purposes, and be used in different ways (Orlikowski, 2000). A practice is a socio-material strategic action carried out in a specific context. Practice is the embodied shared routines and appropriated artefacts of strategy execution (Jarzabkowski et al., 2007; Whittington, 2006). Importantly, practice develops in practical episodes (e.g. communicating strategy), in a specific action, situation, and context, as an expression of cooperation between various practitioners, where material artefacts such as IS/IT play an important role (Huang et al., 2013). These practice episodes may (or may not) follow repeating sequential 'process' patterns (praxis). This is where practice and the strategy process overlap (Whittington, 2007).

Therefore, attention is required to focus on individual practices and their specific aspect (such as practitioners, practices, and praxis), considering the context and the general practice, which is an open strategy (Nicolini, 2009).

4.4 Strategizing challenged by transparency

Over the last decades, with the development of digital technologies, transparency has become the central point of interest of 'good organisations' (Christensen & Cornelissen, 2015; Schnackenberg & Tomlinson, 2016). Organizations faced expectations of greater transparency. However, organizations often release information selectively in a way that does not harm their desired image. In other words, they are skilful practitioners of managed transparency (Christensen & Cheney, 2015; Whittington & Yakis-Douglas, 2020). According to (Ananna & Crawford, 2018), examples of such managed transparency include obfuscated (instead of raw) documents, simplified (instead of facts) transparency reports, well-coordinated press conferences (instead of honest dialogue), or 'manipulated' (instead of verified) numbers. These and other types of managed transparency occur through savvy public relations staff competence, formal regulations such as mandatory confidentiality agreements, or informal pressures. Transparency as an ideal certainly sounds tempting, and organizations willingly declare to adopt such an attitude. In practice, however, transparency is difficult to implement despite advances in information and communication technologies. Organizations, or rather managers, select the information and data they intend to disclose with some caution (Christensen & Cornelissen, 2015).

Advances in information and communication technologies, especially platforms, are an additional incentive to adopt a real transparency attitude. This is possible thanks to frequently mentioned social media tools, such as microblogging sites (e.g. Twitter), social networking sites (e.g. Facebook), personal blogs, webcasts, and publicly accessible wikis. The belief that these new tools and technologies will make transparency possible and that everyone will be able to share data on a large scale, and the belief that democratic circulation and exchange of information and the free creation of new information will be possible, seems to be challenged. Most organizations still use formal control measures, although digital technologies have made this task more difficult. Today, individuals are not dependent on their employers to provide technological infrastructure (anyone can set up a Twitter account). They also cannot be forced to limit their activities to publishing only information on social media that aligns with the organization's needs (e.g. you can always register as an anonymous user and vent your emotions). There are also some advantages here. Unmanaged disclosure of information by organizational members, regardless of their position in the organizational hierarchy, potentially gives access to different points of view. Also, those who are uncomfortable, of which managers are unaware, can be a source of inspiration and reflection. This is the so-called non-management transparency manifested by social media tools. From a different perspective, the development and popularity of social media has created a much greater demand for transparency. However, this means more organizations increasingly adopt managed disclosure forms using digital technologies. However, in these activities, organizations tend to present an idealized self-presentation to their audiences (Reischauer & Ringel, 2023).

Research on open organization (Kornberger et al., 2017; Tkacz, 2012) has mainly focused on the openness that takes place in virtual spaces (von Krogh & Geilenger, 2019) because technology has significantly influenced how openness has become increasingly more possible and standard also in the field of organizing (Puranam et al., 2014).

With a focus on digital and virtual spaces, our main focus is on opensource software development, websites, and online forums (O'Mahony & Bechky, 2008; Puranam et al., 2014; von Hippel & von Krogh, 2003). On the one hand, research has shown how, even in the absence of physical space, knowledge that is difficult to codify, including competencies or experience, can be shared (Faraj et al., 2016). On the other hand, research has shown the limitations of such knowledge sharing in virtual spaces when the principles of openness are challenged by more traditional forms of organizing (Kornberger et al., 2017).

Openness should also be looked at from the perspective of organizational space. From this perspective, openness is mainly mediated by digital or virtual spaces that provide the architecture and possibilities of openness (Chesbrough, 2003; Puranam et al., 2014). However, in open organizing, the consideration of space, particularly physical space, is still recognized mainly in a piecemeal way (Kornberger & Clegg, 2004).

According to Tavakoli et al. (2017), open strategy and similar phenomena question the current understanding of 'organisation' and its boundaries. Open strategy is a new form of organizing that expands organizations through IT.

Moreover, the open strategy is an effect but also an element of transforming the 'open', 'social' and 'network' society enabled by IT (see also Benkler, 2006). Understanding an open strategy requires increasing acceptance and acceptance of IT in all social areas, which is associated with, for example, the widespread use of social media. Nevertheless, it entails corresponding changes in social norms, particularly acceptance that actions and opinions are becoming increasingly transparent. Referring to organizational practices, it is worth emphasizing that they are created by 'reusing' and 'recombining' existing routines from both private and social spaces.

Enthusiasm for transparency and mechanisms for generating transparency, such as freedom of information laws (Roberts, 2005) or voluntary transparency reports (Ananna & Crawford, 2018), have yet to work in practice. Business practice has realized that unmanaged transparency is more effective than unlimited transparency, and at least great hopes are placed on it. Measures within this paradigm virtually allow organizational members to practice disclosing information at their discretion, uninhibited by others, including their superiors. However, the need to implement unmanaged transparency is further supported by the widespread availability of digital technologies, mainly social media tools such as microblogging sites (e.g. Twitter) and wikis. However, research shows inconclusive results in this regard. Some research indicates that unmanaged transparency can positively impact an organization's audience support (Hautz, 2017). Other studies, in turn, draw attention to the risks associated with disclosing confidential information to a potentially critical audience (Albu, 2019).

Existing research on open organizing highlights its contradictions and challenges (Thorén et al., 2018). As can be read from them, openness can sometimes cause opposing tendencies towards closure, that is, limiting or excluding participation (Dobusch et al., 2019), as well as towards secrecy (Costas & Grey, 2014).

Open strategy is a complex and highly dynamic phenomenon, although research emphasises that openness in strategizing also means closure (Dobusch et al., 2019). Taking into account two dimensions of openness, that is, transparency and inclusion (Hautz et al., 2017; Whittington et al., 2011), the dynamics of openness were discovered by examining it in terms of who should be included or excluded in the strategy process at the organizational level (Vaara et al., 2019) and interorganizational (Seidl & Werle, 2018); what type of information should be shared and to what extent (Malhotra et al., 2017); and how openness can be promoted or hindered (Whittington & Yakis-Douglas, 2020).

A critical study on open strategy was conducted by Dobusch and colleagues (2019), who analyzed open strategy practices as an embodiment of ideals of organizational openness. They examined how the use of wikis promoted the involvement of internal and external actors in the organization by allowing them to access sensitive information. As virtual spaces for open strategizing, wikis represent a collaborative space of interconnected websites where all actors can modify the text in content and structure (Dobusch et al., 2019). However, this study showed how openness in shaping strategy content depended on closure forms. Additionally, Dobusch and colleagues (2019) emphasize that openness should be interpreted more than just a lack of organizational structure because unstructured openness may lead to exclusion in strategizing.

However, even when an open organization accepts a more significant and more extensive exchange of information and ideas, researchers have raised concerns about information overload, which may limit the ability of individuals and groups to process these ideas productively (Hautz et al., 2017). Indeed, the amount of information generated by open organization processes can be overwhelming. Excessive amounts of information, as reported by (Luedicke et al., 2017), can lead to mental and emotional fatigue, make it difficult to extract relevant information that guides idea generation and action, have a destructive impact on participants' involvement and motivation, and lead to many competing interpretations of available information.

From research on open strategy, information overload can be managed in practice. For example, researchers have identified practices such as controlling agenda-setting and selective participation (Luedicke et al., 2017; Stieger et al., 2012), pragmatic closure of participation to move the process forward (Dobusch et al., 2019), and the strategic management of impression management by moving from dialogue and inclusion to broadcasting practices (Gegenhuber & Dobusch, 2017). As can be readily seen, this research focuses on how leaders can exercise control over open processes and does not directly address the challenge of managing information overload over time for diverse participants, especially in the absence of formal control.

Additional insights into the diversity and vast amount of digital content that leaders may have to manage are provided by research on protest networks, digital technology, and social movements. Information overload is the main challenge here, which can be dealt with, for example, by cataloguing digital content (Fotopoulou & Couldry, 2015).

It is also worth referring to the positive aspects of openness, which can be associated with the need to share knowledge in online communities. So far, such recognition has focused on the individual level of analysis (Butler, 2001). Lingo's (2023) research focusing on emerging collective processes shows that the process perspective becomes important when individual participants need more information about the identity, motivation, and actual knowledge base of the people who provide them with answers. This perspective places less emphasis on individual sources of information and more on the emerging dynamics that enable and constrain the circulation and validation of misleading knowledge. This approach allows for identifying sequences in an open online platform that facilitates or hinders knowledge sharing.

Lingo's (2023) study also revealed an unexpectedly positive aspect of trolling for open organizing – research on trolling mainly points to its many harmful consequences. Surprisingly, Lingo reveals that trolling can prompt others to focus their discussions in an open online environment. Trolling is extreme behaviour that can cause events to change. A process perspective will reveal that controversial positions or rude language may prompt others to try to repair the discussion and get it back on track. In open online platforms, where it is impossible to verify all posts and the topics discussed are complex, trolling may trigger compensatory strivings for more likely answers.

Employees' acceptance of digitalization must also be considered when using openness and promoting transparency and inclusiveness (Hwang et al., 2016).

4.5 Capability perspective

Success in digital transformation is attributed to the ability of companies to shift to new models of thinking about competition, develop supportive digital routines, and introduce new organizational structures in a way that allows these elements to support each other. In short, digital transformation is not just about adopting digital technology but also about shaping how it is perceived, adopted, and used and building supportive digital routines and new organizational forms (Volberda et al., 2021). For this reason, explanations relating to the essence of organizational capabilities, and in particular dynamic capabilities, become important from the perspective of an open form of strategizing.

Organizational capabilities occupy an important place in the literature on the subject. Their importance is directly related to the development of the resource-based approach by Williamson (1991), which is one of the approaches in strategic management used as the epistemological basis for understanding, conceptualizing, and implementing the dynamic resource-based approach in organizational research (Helfat & Peteraf, 2003).

Resource logic is valid in this respect because it raises the importance of idiosyncratic resources and organizational capabilities that influence the effects achieved by organizations (Barney, 1991).

According to Amit and Schoemaker (1993), organizational capabilities mean the potential to arrange resources according to the assumed organizational goals using their combinations and organizational processes. Organizational capabilities are directly related to the ability to use resources (Grant, 1991). Additionally, it is emphasized that organizational capabilities are characterized by regularity in obtaining results (Loasby, 2010).

The trend of research on organizational capabilities consists of many of research approaches focusing on the behaviour and organization of a company (e.g. Collis, 1994; Helfat et al., 2007). As Foss (2001) points out, this trend includes research on capabilities, dynamic capabilities, and competencies. Also, it falls within the interests of the resource-based approach and the evolutionary theory of the company, in which routines are the object of research.

Routines and capabilities are central constructs found in many different research areas. Organizational capabilities are located, for example, in human resources, but also in organizational routines (Nelson & Winter, 1982; Cohen et al., 1996; Dosi et al., 2000). Moreover, Pentland and Rueter's (1994) definition of routines is consistent with the concept of capabilities. For this reason, an organization is more than the sum of its resources, more than the sum of the abilities of individual, organizational participants (Winter, 2003), and, beyond doubt, more than the sum of organizational routines (Katkalo et al., 2010).

Winter (2003) explicitly states that capabilities are a set of routines or higher-level routines. Routines, in turn, are learned, highly structured, repeatable behaviours partially grounded in implicit knowledge and specific goals. Capabilities indicate how effectively routines are performed relative to competitors (Nelson & Winter, 1982). Capabilities are a set of routines (Winter, 2003).

Helfat and Peteraf (2003) argue that capabilities reside in routines; therefore, organizational activities can only be understood once they have been practised or routinized and function in a proven manner. This is also confirmed in other studies, where it is emphasized that dynamic capabilities are exemplified in ad hoc problem solving (Winter, 2003). It is also worth emphasising that in the study of both organizational capabilities and organizational routines, the role of embedding these constructs in the organizational context and the historically conditioned path of development of these entities is emphasized (Trentin et al., 2015), which is an additional argument for that both changing established routines and changing capabilities is a big challenge for the organization.

Many studies show that organizational capabilities are built on organizational routines (Dosi et al., 2000; Nelson & Winter, 1982; Winter, 2003). Grant (1991) puts this point squarely by stating that organizational capabilities are simply routines or a set of interacting routines.

Dynamic capabilities are a response to the dynamics of the context, and organizational routines are the basic components of these capabilities (Winter, 2003) and exemplify the possibility of reconfiguring and changing the resource base.

Dynamic capabilities are the capabilities of an organization to integrate, build, and reconfigure internal and external competencies to meet the requirements of a rapidly changing environment (Teece et al., 1997). Competencies, in the definition of dynamic capabilities, represent a bundle of resources, or organization-specific assets, that are embedded in an integrated bundle of individuals and groups (Teece et al., 1997). Competencies are understood as the ability to integrate and manage available resources or assets specific to the organization.

Dynamic capabilities focus on organizational routines and organizational and management processes. As a result, the idea of dynamic capabilities refers, on the one hand, to results and, on the other hand, is built from many elements, among which routines, the role of managers, the dynamics of the environment, and internal organizational processes become central points. Dynamic capabilities are usually rooted in organizational processes and routines that allow the organization to adapt to changing conditions by reconfiguring the organizational resource base (Pavlou & El Sawy, 2011). Teece et al. (1997) also claim that processes, positions, and paths become important as unique internal routines serve the strategy.

It is difficult to determine what the dynamics of dynamic capabilities are clearly. In addition to the previously indicated views, others fall into this group and justify that higher-order abilities are simply dynamic routines exemplifying higher-order abilities (Lei et al., 1996). Dynamic capabilities refer to higher-order capabilities, that is, routines that modify existing routines (Athreye et al., 2009). As a result, the routinized nature of dynamic capabilities is exposed (Zollo, Winter, 2002; Winter, 2003; Felin & Foss, 2009), allowing us to assume that dynamic capabilities manifest specific routines.

Dunning and Lundan (2010) explain that the diffusion of new routines and good practices is an important outcome of organizational dynamic capabilities. Over time, such capabilities are codified and diffuse, which means they cease to be a unique advantage of the organization in which they were created. They are not ad hoc improvisations in response to changed conditions but incorporate an element of routine in solving specific problems. Specific practices can be isolated and articulated into routines, becoming good practices but not dynamic capabilities. The transfer of new routines is likely to be limited because they are 'sticky', to use Szulanski's rhetoric (Szulanski, 1996). After all, they incorporate tacit knowledge that we cannot fully articulate. Another reason for developing new routines is their context dependence.

Competencies/abilities are similar to routines. If a company fixates on certain competencies/capabilities, it loses flexibility and the ability to respond to changing contextual features. Suppose specific competencies have ensured success over a long period. In that case, there is a tendency to oversimplify operational procedures and to be unable to notice deviations and negative feedback, which is called the Icarus paradox (Miller, 1992) or the 'capabilities trap' (Hannan & Freeman, 1984). Consequently, the winning pattern becomes the losing pattern.

Existing routines may significantly limit the open model of strategizing. Still, the development of digital technologies, particularly social media, shapes new individual routines, which, however, are incorporated by the organization's members. Therefore, the routines on which organizational capabilities are based require change and, as a result, the development of new organizational capabilities.

In particular, social media increases transparency and inclusion in organizational strategizing, expanding involvement in creating strategy content and participant engagement. However, more than relying solely on opinions posted on social media is required to implement an open strategy approach. Instead, social media users' opinions initially lead to tensions between the participatory nature of the technology and existing management practices. Ultimately, these tensions foster the development of new internal capabilities that allow for structured consideration of these views within the organization. These new organizational capabilities are reflexivity (Baptista et al., 2017).

Social media help shape new types and patterns of communication and interaction within the organization, which may influence its structure, management, and organizational principles (Leonardi et al., 2013; Treem & Leonardi, 2012). Wider participation in strategic activities via social media may conflict with existing formal structures and norms in organizations. However, organizations learn to manage and use this feedback, becoming inherently more reflective and able to create an environment where greater participation and involvement in the shaping and direction of strategy becomes more natural. This happens when strategy practitioners reflect on action systems (Gorli et al., 2015; Wilson & Jarzabkowski, 2004). Hence, social media stimulates reflexivity, which is perceived as a new organizational capability. Including social media in the functioning of organizations means that opinions and participation are a structural part of the organization.

Reflexivity is a social concept meaning the ability to analyze oneself in thinking and acting. At the individual level, it means introspection and self-awareness. Still, from a social perspective, it concerns interaction with others in the context of the established norms of a given social group. In organizations, this ability requires information systems and addresses the ability of employees to apply practical reflexivity (Cunliffe, 2002). In this way, employees receive structural conditions in which they can play an active role in creating and transforming organizational processes (Gorli et al., 2015).

Consequently, organizations with low reflexivity allow only little influence on changing the established social structure. In turn, organizations with high reflexivity enable a high level of influence by individuals and shape the norms and structures of their own environment, which additionally leads to understanding and shaping organizational practices. This, in turn, allows individuals to influence organizations, constituting a significant breakthrough from conventional approaches to strategy and organization.

4.6   Openness and the (changing) role of the upper echelon

To some extent, an open strategy contradicts conventional strategic practices in which senior managers maintain strong positions (Brielmaier & Friesl, 2021). Moreover, it is not evident that senior managers adopt, accept, or tolerate open strategy in some form precisely because of their previously dominant role in the strategic process (Belmondo & Sargis-Roussel, 2023; Whittington & Yakis-Douglas, 2020). As a result, such open strategic practices need to be aligned with the interests of senior managers, who may act against the integration of open strategy into the strategic process (Hautz et al., 2017). In this context, the commitment of corporate elites to an open strategy has even been described as 'utopian' (Vaara et al., 2019).

However, the tendency to open strategic processes on the one hand and the concerns of senior managers on the other (Hautz et al., 2017) draw attention to a process that is called open strategy infiltration and means the inclusion of an open strategy into strategic processes, taking place behind the backs of senior managers' level (Vaara et al., 2019). Whether introduced by senior managers or emerging from the bottom, open strategy initiatives are transient phenomena (Gegenhuber & Dobusch, 2017). In turn, the infiltration of an open strategy can incorporate the exercise of transparency and inclusiveness in the strategic process in a long-term and more sustainable way and is an important contribution to the general trend of opening strategic processes (Vaara et al., 2019; Whittington & Yakis-Douglas, 2020)

The open strategy may also permeate the strategic process through a partially unnoticed drift of strategic practices. Based on research, Stjerne et al. (2023) found that organizational members realize this drift by accommodating and legitimizing the exercise of transparency and inclusiveness in the strategic process. This research shows that an open strategy can become part of the strategic process through both managed and unmanaged processes (Whittington & Yakis-Douglas, 2020). In particular, Stjerne et al. (2023) view open strategy infiltration as a drift in strategic practices that induces and escapes senior managers' attention. An open strategy becomes part of the strategic process as managers and employees' practice transparency and inclusiveness in their strategy work. As a result, senior managers even ultimately contribute to the reproduction of open strategy in the strategy process by responding to this drift in strategic practices through goal-based rationalization and procedural renegotiation.

Both the infiltration of open strategy and the associated drift of strategic practices embody the praxis exposed in the strategy-as-practice approach. These findings are significant because they identify a role for senior managers in opening the strategic process that differs significantly from that promoted in prior research. In particular, an open strategy implies at least partial loss of control over the strategic process. This is because individuals outside the strategic process may inadvertently 'practice' transparency and inclusivity in the strategic process.

Of course, a formalized strategy can still be managed top-down in many organizations, but the digital context leaves no doubt. In particular, social media pressures the strategy process to become more open to informal activities. This is particularly important as the younger generation of digital natives (Helsper & Eynon, 2009) become dominant due to their ability to use social media to engage and interact with others (Tams et al., 2014) and share knowledge (Morton et al., 2015). The participatory nature of social media is changing the distribution and patterns of communication (Huang et al., 2015). Furthermore, social media are integral to knowledge management (Von Krogh, 2012), knowledge reuse (Majchrzak et al., 2013), distributed leadership (Sutanto et al., 2011), and in facilitating interaction and internal collaboration (Razmerita et al., 2014). However, the greater visibility of what others know through social media creates conditions for using knowledge in new ways and promotes learning as a process (Leonardi, 2014). This is important for strategy because social media highlights the role and voice of each organization member, providing a platform for engagement and participation (Haefliger et al., 2011).

They can, therefore, increase the reach and richness of creating and implementing a strategy, but they also often replace traditional forms of communication of an existing strategy.

Open strategy is a practice that opens the highest level of the organization, allowing for broad participation in the discussion, creation, and decision-making regarding strategy. However, more is needed to know how this opening changes power relations between owners, managers, employees, and other organizational stakeholders. How does it affect the identities of those involved – for example, whether the role of the CEO shifts from strategy maker to strategy manager?

References

Albu, O. B. (2019). Dis/ordering: The use of information and communication technologies by human rights civil society organizations. In C. Vásquez & T. Kuhn (Eds.), *Dis/organization as communication: Exploring the disordering, disruptive and chaotic properties of communication* (pp. 151–171). Routledge.

Amit, R., & Schoemaker, P. J. H. (1993). Strategic assets and organizational rent. *Strategic Management Journal, 14*(1), 33–46.

Ananna, M., & Crawford, K. (2018). Seeing without knowing: Limitations of the transparency ideal and its application to algorithmic accountability. *New Media & Society, 20*, 973–989.

Athreye, S., Kale, D., & Ramani, S. V. (2009). Experimentation with strategy and the evolution of dynamic capability in the Indian pharmaceutical sector. *Industrial and Corporate Change, 18*(4), 729–759.

Baptista, J., Wilson, A. D., Galliers, R. D., & Bynghall, S. (2017). Social media and the emergence of reflexiveness as a new capability for open strategy. *Long Range Planning, 50*, 322–336.

Barney, J. (1991). Firm resources and sustained competitive advantage. *Journal of Management, 17*(1), 99–120.

Belmondo, C., & Sargis-Roussel, C. (2023). The political dynamics of opening participation in strategy: The role of strategy specialists' legitimacy and disposition to openness. *Organization Studies, 44*(4), 613–635.

Benkler, Y. (2006). *The wealth of networks*. Yale University Press.

Brielmaier, C., & Friesl, M. (2021). Pulled in all directions: Open strategy participation as an attention contest. *Strategic Organization, 21*(3), 709–720.

Butler, B. S. (2001). Membership size, community activity, and sustainability: A resource-based model of online social structures. *Information Systems Research, 12*(4), 346–362.

Chesbrough, H. (2003). Open platform innovation: Creating value from internal and external innovation. *Intel Technology Journal, 7*, 5–9.

Christensen, L. T., & Cheney, G. (2015). Peering into transparency: Challenging ideals, proxies, and organizational practices. *Communication Theory, 25*, 70–90.

Christensen, L. T., & Cornelissen, J. (2015). Organizational transparency as myth and metaphor. *European Journal of Social Theory, 18*, 132–149.

Cohen, M. D., Burkhart, R., Dosi, G., Egidi, M., Marengo, L., Warglien, M., & Winter, S. (1996). Routines and other recurring action; Patterns of organisations: Contemporary research issues. *Industrial and Corporate Change, 5*(3), 653–698.

Collis, D. J. (1994). Research note: How valuable are organizational capabilities. *Strategic Management Journal, 15*(1), 143–152.

Costas, J., & Grey, C. (2014). Bringing secrecy into the open: Towards a theorization of the social processes of organizational secrecy. *Organization Studies, 35*, 1423–1447.

Cunliffe, A. L. (2002). Reflexive dialogical practice in management learning. *Management Learning, 33*(1), 35–61.

Dobusch, L., & Gegenhuber, T. (2015). Making an impression with open strategy: Transparency and engagement on corporate blogs. *Academy of Management Proceedings, 1*.

Dobusch L., Dobusch L., & Müller-Seitz, G. (2019). Closing for the benefit of openness? The case of Wikimedia's open strategy process. *Organization Studies, 40*(3), 343–370.

Dosi, G., Nelson, R. R., & Winter, S. G. (2000). Introduction: The nature and dynamics of organisational capabilities. In G. Dosi, R. R. Nelson & S. G. Winter (Eds.), *The nature and dynamics of organisational capabilities* (pp. 1–22). Oxford University Press.

Dunning, J. H., & Lundan, S. M. (2010). The institutional origins of dynamic capabilities in multinational enterprises -super-†. *Industrial and Corporate Change, 19*(4), 1225–1246.

Eisenhardt, K. M., & Martin, J. A. (2000). Dynamic capabilities what are they. *Strategic Management Journal, 21*, 1105–1121.

El Sawy, O., Amsinck, H., Kraemmergaard, P., & Lerbech, V. A. (2016). How LEGO built the foundations and enterprise capabilities for digital leadership. *MIS Quarterly Executive, 15*(2), Article 5.

Faraj, S., von Krogh, G., Monteiro, E., & Lakhani, K. R. (2016). Special section introduction: Online community as space for knowledge flows. *Information Systems Research, 27*, 668–684.

Felin, T., & Foss, N. J. (2005). Strategic organization: A field in search of micro-foundations. *Strategic Organization, 3*(4), 441–455.

Felin, T., & Foss, N. J. (2009). Organizational routines and capabilities: Historical drift and a course-correction toward microfoundations. *Scandinavian Journal of Management, 25*(2), 157–167.

Foss, N. J. (2001). The problem with bounded rationality: Ruminations on behavioral assumptions in the theory of the firm. In *DRUID Conference*, 12–15 June 2001, Aalborg.

Fotopoulou, A., & Couldry, N. (2015). Telling the story of the stories: Online content curation and digital engagement. *Information, Communication & Society, 18*(2), 235–249.

Gavetti, G., & Levinthal, D. (2000). Looking Forward and Looking Backward: Cognitive and Experiential Search. *Administrative Science Quarterly, 45*(1), 113–137.

Gegenhuber, T., & Dobusch, L. (2017). Making an impression through openness: How open strategy-making practices change in the evolution of new ventures. *Long Range Planning, 50,* 337–354.

Gorli, M., Nicolini, D., & Scaratti, G. (2015). Reflexivity in practice: Tools and conditions for developing organizational authorship. *Human Relations, 68*(8), 1347–1375.

Grant, R. M. (1991). The resource-based theory of competitive advantage: Implications for strategy formulation. *California Management Review,* 114–135.

Haefliger, S., Monteiro, E., Foray, D., & von Krogh, G. (2011). Social software and strategy. *Long Range Planning, 44*(5–6), 297–316.

Hannan, M. T., & Freeman, J. (1984). Structural inertia and organizational change. *American Sociological Review, 49*(2), 149–164.

Hansen, H. K., & Flyverbom, M. (2015). The politics of transparency and the calibration of knowledge in the digital age. *Organization, 22,* 872–889.

Hautz, J. (2017). Opening up the strategy process – A network perspective. *Management Decision, 55,* 1956–1983.

Helfat, C. E., Finkelstein, S., Mitchell, W., Peteraf, M. A., Singh, H., Teece, D. J., & Winter, S. G. (2007). *Dynamic capabilities: Understanding strategic change and organizations,* Blackwell.

Helfat, C. E., & Peteraf, M. A. (2003). The dynamic resource-based view: Capability lifecycles. *Strategic Management Journal, 24*(10), 997–1010.

Helsper, E., & Eynon, R. (2009). Digital natives: Where is the evidence? *British Educational Research Journal, 36*(3), 1–18.

Hodgkinson, G. P., Whittington, R., Johnson, G., & Schwarz, M. (2006). The role of strategy workshops in strategy development processes: Formality, communication, co-ordination and inclusion. *Long Range Planning, 39*(5), 479–496.

Huang, J., Baptista, J., & Galliers, R. D. (2013). Reconceptualizing rhetorical practices in organizations: The impact of social media on internal communications. *Information & Management, 50*(2–3), 112–124.

Huang, J., Baptista, J., & Newell, S. (2015). Communicational ambidexterity as a new capability to manage social media communication within organizations. *Journal of Strategic Information Systems, 24*(2), 49–64.

Huang, J., Newell, S., Huang, J., & Pan, S.-L. (2014). Site-shifting as the source of ambidexterity: Empirical insights from the field of ticketing. *Journal of Strategic Information Systems, 23*(1), 29–44.

Hwang, Y., Al-Arabiat, M., & Shin, D.-H. (2016). Understanding technology acceptance in a mandatory environment: A literature review. *Information Development, 32*(4), 1266–1283.

Jarzabkowski, P., Balogun, J., & Seidl, D. (2007). Strategizing: The challenges of practice perspective. *Human Relations, 60*(1), 5–27.

Jarzabkowski, P., Burke, G., & Spee, P. (2015). Constructing spaces for strategic work: A multimodal perspective. *British Journal of Management, 26,* 26–47.

Jarzabkowski, P., Kaplan, S., Seidl, D., & Whittington, R. (2016). On the risk of studying practices in isolation: Linking what, who, and how in strategy research. *Strategic Organization, 14*, 248–259.

Katkalo, V. S., Pitelis, C. N., & Teece, D. J. (2010). Introduction: On the nature and scope of dynamic capabilities. *Industrial and Corporate Change, 19*(4), 1175–1186.

Kornberger, M., & Clegg, S. R. (2004). Bringing space back in organizing the generative building. *Organization Studies, 25*, 1095–1114.

Kornberger, M., Meyer, R. E., Brandtner, C., & Höllerer, M. A. (2017). When bureaucracy meets the crowd: Studying 'open government' in the Vienna city administration. *Organization Studies, 38*, 179–200.

Lei, D., Hitt, M. A., & Bettis, R. (1996). Dynamic core competences through meta-learning and strategic context. *Journal of Management, 22*(4), 549–569.

Leonardi, P. M. (2014). Social media, knowledge sharing, and innovation: Toward a theory of communication visibility. *Information Systems Research, 25*(4), 796–816.

Leonardi, P. M., Huysman, M., & Steinfield, C. (2013). Enterprise social media: Definition, history, and prospects for the study of social technologies in organizations. *Journal of Computer-Mediated Communication, 19*(1), 1–19.

Lingo, E. L. (2023). Digital curation and creative brokering: Managing information overload in open organizing. *Organization Studies, 44*(1), 105–133.

Loasby, B. J. (2010). Capabilities and strategy: Problems and prospects. *Industrial and Corporate Change, 19*(4), 1301–1316.

Luedicke, M. K., Husemann, K. C., Furnari, S., & Ladstaetter, F. (2017). Radically open strategizing: How premium cola collective takes open strategy to the extreme. *Long Range Planning, 50*(3), 371–384.

Majchrzak, A.,Wagner, C., & Yates, D. (2013). The impact of shaping on knowledge for organizational improvement with wikis. *MIS Quarterly, 37*(2), 455–A412.

Miller, D. (1992). The icarus paradox: How exceptional companies bring about their own downfall. *Business Horizons, 35*(1), 24–35.

Morton, Josh, Alexander D. Wilson, & Louise Cooke. 2019. "Collaboration and Knowledge Sharing in Open Strategy Initiatives". figshare. https://hdl.handle.net/2134/18621.

Nelson, R. R., & Winter, S. G. (1982). *An evolutionary theory of economic change.* Belknap Press.

Nicolini, D. (2009). Zooming in and out: Studying practices by switching theoretical lenses and trailing connections. *Organization Studies, 30*(12), 1391–1418.

O'Mahony, S., & Bechky, B. A. (2008). Boundary organizations: Enabling collaboration among unexpected allies. *Administrative Science Quarterly, 53*, 422–459.

Orlikowski, W. J. (2000). Using technology and constituting structures: A practice lens for studying technology in organizations. *Organization Science, 11*(4), 404–428.

Pavlou, P. A., & El Sawy, O. A. (2011). Understanding the elusive black box of dynamic capabilities. *Decision Sciences, 42*(1), 239–273.

Pentland, B. T., & Rueter, H. H. (1994). Organizational routines as grammars of action. *Administrative Science Quarterly, 39*(3), 484–510.

Pittz, T. G., & Adler, T. (2016). An exemplar of open strategy: Decision-making within multi-sector collaborations. *Management Decision, 54*(7), 1595–1614.

Prashantham, S., & Healey, M. P. (2022). Strategy as practice research: Reflections on its rationale, approach, and contributions. *Journal of Management Studies, 59*, 1–17. https://doi.org/10.1111/joms.12862

Puranam, P., Alexy, O., & Reitzig, M. (2014). What's "new" about new forms of organizing? *Academy of Management Review, 39*, 162–180.

Razmerita, L., Kirchner, K., & Nabeth, T. (2014). Social media in organizations: Leveraging personal and collective knowledge processes. *Journal of Organizational Computing and Electronic Commerce, 24*(1), 74–93.

Reckwitz, A. (2002). Towards a theory of social practice: A development in cultural theorizing. *European Journal of Social Theory, 5*(2), 243–263.

Reischauer, G., & Ringel, L. (2023). Unmanaged transparency in a digital society: Swiss army knife or double-edged sword? *Organization Studies, 44*(1), 77–104.

Roberts, A. S. (2005). Spin control and freedom of information: Lessons for the United Kingdom from Canada. *Public Administration, 83*, 1–23.

Schatzki, T. R. (1996). *Social practices: A wittgensteinian approach to human activity and the social.* Cambridge University Press.

Schatzki, T. R. (1997). Practices and actions: A Wittgensteinian critique of Bourdieu and Giddens. *Philosophy of the Social Sciences, 27*(3), 284.

Schnackenberg, A. K., & Tomlinson, E. C. (2016). Organizational transparency: A new perspective on managing trust in organization-stakeholder relationships. *Journal of Management, 42*, 1784–1810.

Seidl, D., & Werle, F. (2018). Inter-organizational sensemaking in the face of strategic meta-problems: Requisite variety and dynamics of participation. *Strategic Management Journal, 39*, 830–858.

Stein, M.-K., Newell, S., Wagner, E. L., & Galliers, R. D. (2014). Felt quality of sociomaterial relations: Introducing emotions into sociomaterial theorizing. *Information Organization, 24*(3), 156–175.

Stieger, D., Matzler, K., Chatterjee, S., & Ladstaetter-Fussenegger, F. (2012). Democratizing strategy: How crowdsourcing can be used for strategy dialogues. *California Management Review, 54*, 44–68.

Stjerne, I., Geraldi, J., & Wenzel, M. (2023). Strategic practice drift: How open strategy infiltrates the strategy process. *Journal of Management Studies*, https://doi.org/10.1111/joms.12895

Sutanto, J., Tan, C.-H., Battistini, B., & Phang, C. W. (2011). Emergent leadership in virtual collaboration settings: A social network analysis approach. *Long Range Planning, 44*(5), 421–439.

Szulanski, G. (1996). Exploring internal stickiness impediments to the transfer of best practice within the firm. *Strategic Management Journal, 17*, 27–43.

Tams, S., Grover, V., & Thatcher, J. (2014). Modern information technology in an old workforce: Toward a strategic research agenda. *The Journal of Strategic Information Systems, 23*(4), 284–304.

Tavakoli, A., Schlagwein, D., & Schoder, D. (2017). Open strategy: Literature review, re-analysis of cases and conceptualisation as a practice. *The Journal of Strategic Information Systems, 26*(3), 163–184.

Teece, D. J., Pisano, G., & Shuen, A. (1997). Dynamic capabilities and strategic management. *Strategic Management Journal, 18*(7), 509–533.

Thorén, C., Ågerfalk, P. J., & Rolandsson, B. (2018). Voicing the puppet: Accommodating unresolved institutional tensions in digital open practices. *Organization Studies, 39*, 923–945.

Tkacz, N. (2012). From open source to open government: A critique of open politics. *Ephemera: Theory and Politics in Organization, 12*, 386–405.

Treem, J., & Leonardi, P. (2012). Social media use in organizations: Exploring the affordances of visibility, editability, persistence, and association. *Communication Yearbook, 36*, 143–189.

Trentin, A., Forza, C., & Perin, E. (2015). Embeddedness and path dependence of organizational capabilities for mass customization and green management: A longitudinal case study in the machinery industry. *International Journal of Production Economics, 169*(C), 253–276.

Vaara, E., Rantakari, A., & Holstein, J. (2019). Participation research and open strategy. In D. Seidl, R. Whittington & G. Von Krogh (Eds.), *Cambridge handbook of open strategy* (pp. 27–40). Cambridge University Press.

Vaara, E., & Whittington, R. (2012). Strategy-as-practice: Taking social practices seriously. *Academy of Management Annals, 6*(1), 285–336.

Volberda, H. W., Khanagha, S., Baden-Fuller, C., Mihalache, O. R., & Birkinshaw, J. (2021). Strategizing in a digital world: Overcoming cognitive barriers, reconfiguring routines and introducing new organizational forms. *Long Range Planning, 54*(5), 102110.

Von Hippel, E., & Von Krogh, G. (2003). Open source software and the "private-collective" innovation model: Issues for organization science. *Organization Science, 14*, 209–223.

Von Krogh, G. (2012). How does social software change knowledge management? Toward a strategic research agenda. *The Journal of Strategic Information Systems, 21*, 154–164.

Von Krogh, G., & Geilenger, N. (2019). Open innovation and open strategy: Epistemic and design dimensions. In D. Seidl, R. Whittington & G. Von Krogh (Eds.), *The Cambridge handbook of open strategy* (pp. 41–58). Cambridge University Press.

Whittington, R. (2006). Completing the practice turn in strategy research. *Organization Studies, 27*, 613–634.

Whittington, R. (2007). Strategy practice and strategy process: Family differences and the sociological eye. *Organization Studies, 28*(10), 1575–1586.

Whittington, R. (2012). Big strategy/small strategy. *Strategic Organization, 10*(3), 263–268.

Whittington, R. (2015). The massification of strategy. *British Journal of Management, 26*, 13–16.

Whittington, R., Cailluet, L., & Yakis-Douglas, B. (2011). Opening strategy: Evolution of a precarious profession. *British Journal of Management, 22*, 531–544.

Whittington, R., & Yakis-Douglas, B. (2020). The grand challenge of corporate control: Opening strategy to the normative pressures of networked professionals. *Organization Theory, 1,* 1–19.

Williamson, O. E. (1991). Comparative economic organization: The analysis of discrete structural alternatives. *Administrative Science Quarterly, 36*(2), 269–296.

Wilson, D. C., & Jarzabkowski, P. (2004). Thinking and acting strategically: New challenges for interrogating strategy. *European Management Journal, 1*(1), 14–20.

Winter, S. (2003). Understanding dynamic capabilities. *Strategic Management Journal, 24*(10), 991–995.

Zollo, M., & Winter, S. (2002). Deliberate learning and the evolution of dynamic capabilities. *Organization Science, 13*(3), 339–351.

5 Digital technologies as drivers of strategizing practices

5.1 Open strategy drivers

Many factors will be crucial in determining how open the open strategizing process is. However, the reasons for this openness should be primarily sought in digital transformation and, ultimately, in digital work. Digital transformation changes everything, societies and businesses, and is characterized by the space of social, mobile, cloud, and smart technologies (Alter, 2014).

One of the primary challenges confronting contemporary businesses lies in digitalization, a sociotechnical process that facilitates the evolution of new organizational procedures, business models, and commercial offerings (Brynjolfsson & McAfee, 2014). This process compels firms to adapt to emerging organizational forms and acquire the requisite skill sets to remain viable and pertinent in the context of a digital landscape.

Morton et al. (2022) present a comprehensive assessment and research agenda focused on the 'nexus' between information systems and strategy practice. They introduce 'digital strategizing' to elucidate the intricate relationship between digital technologies and individuals across different organizational levels, encompassing processes that shape, convey, implement, host, and support strategy. Digital organizations empower employees with digital literacy to regularly engage with digital technologies in their professional lives (Davison & Ou, 2017). For instance, email serves as the officially sanctioned tool for both internal and external communication, while access to social media applications is restricted.

Information Technology is intentionally utilized to facilitate the implementation of a concept known as open strategizing (Whittington et al., 2011; Morton et al., 2020). This involves strategists actively participating in digital processes that digitize strategy formulation (Amrollahi & Rowlands, 2018). Through digital work, strategists embrace more inclusive practices, involving a broader array of individuals in developing strategy. Additionally, these digital tools promote transparency, making strategic information more accessible and visible (Tavakoli et al., 2017). Research on open strategizing illustrates how IT fosters a strategic dialogue with various stakeholders, contributing valuable insights to the overall strategy development (Amrollahi & Rowlands, 2017).

DOI: 10.4324/9781003424772-5

Consequently, a central focus within open strategizing revolves around utilising Information Technology (Morton et al., 2020). This emphasis is substantiated by studies highlighting the application of social media, ideation platforms, and web-based questionnaires (Baptista et al., 2017; Tavakoli et al., 2017). In examining open strategizing, attention is directed towards IT-enabled practices, specifically the digital work undertaken by top managers in the context of open strategizing. Indeed, within the Information Systems domain, Tavakoli and colleagues (2017) have contributed to the theoretical advancement of open strategizing by elucidating that information technology plays a crucial role in either supplementing or replacing traditional analog strategy work, thereby facilitating instances of openness.

This emphasizes the strong collaboration between open strategizing and Information Technology, highlighting its potential to impact both strategy development and organizational transformation (Hautz et al., 2017).

Integrating Information Technology and social media introduces novel capabilities that can significantly enhance engagement in strategic processes. Strategists adapt their methodologies by integrating or substituting traditional 'analog' strategizing with digital approaches (Baptista et al., 2017). Baptista and colleagues underscore organizations' importance in cultivating reflexivity to utilize social media for effective open strategizing.

Information technologies are reshaping the character of work within organizations, prompting the restructuring of work methodologies. These novel work practices collectively fall under the 'digital work' (Orlikowski & Scott, 2016). Various facets of digital work have been scrutinized, encompassing the role of web 2.0 tools in mediating knowledge sharing (Simeonova, 2018), the emergence of digitally enabled jobs in offshoring work (Sandeep & Ravishankar, 2015), the interplay between human and computer work practices (Richter et al., 2018), and the dynamics within organizations facing digital challenges (Davison & Ou, 2017). However, the digital work undertaken by strategists still needs to be explored. However, the exploration of digital work holds significant implications for organizations and workers alike.

Open strategizing involves finding a balance between the social aspects of strategy and organizing and recognizing technology's role in strategy work. It is effectively realized when organizations integrate internal and external stakeholders into the strategizing process, thereby accessing fresh insights that contribute to strategic direction and organizational transformation (Whittington et al., 2011; Hautz et al., 2017).

Volberda et al. (2021) propose a framework for strategizing within the contemporary digital competitive landscape, emphasizing the significance of the interplay between (1) the cognitive challenges managers encounter in comprehending the new digital realm and envisioning innovative digital business models, (2) the imperative to adapt and extend digital routines, and (3) the establishment of new organizational forms better suited for creating value and gaining a competitive edge.

Researchers have initiated the identification of factors facilitating OS, such as essential capabilities (Baptista et al., 2017). For instance, Schroll and Mild (2012) have pinpointed commonly studied factors that are potential determinants of openness, categorizing them into organizational capabilities and environmental conditions. In this context, we emphasize managers' commitment to implementing open practices and active participation.

In general, open strategizing offers two primary advantages. Firstly, it facilitates the dissemination of valuable strategic knowledge across various levels of a firm, aiding in the execution of a strategy (e.g. Plotnikova et al., 2021; Stieger et al., 2012). Secondly, open strategizing initiatives enable the harnessing of expertise from diverse actors, thereby holding the potential for developing superior strategies (e.g. Hautz et al., 2017). Given the bounded rationality of actors, the top management team may be unable to consider all potential options to select the 'perfect' strategy. Open strategizing addresses this limitation by expanding the array of options through the inclusion of contributions from internal and external stakeholders in the strategy process (e.g. Mack & Szulanski, 2017).

The prerequisite for realizing the benefits of open strategizing practices may seem almost self-evident: participation. Utilizing distributed knowledge to formulate superior strategies assumes that actors possessing this knowledge invest their attention in sharing it. Despite its significance, only a few scholars have distinguished participation and inclusion (Plotnikova et al., 2021; Stieger et al., 2012). In the emerging literature on open strategizing, three approaches to participation currently exist: participation as a consequence of inclusion, participation as inclusion with lower intensity, and participation as an inherent challenge of open strategizing.

Top managers' commitment to an open strategy is not a foregone conclusion (Belmondo & Sargis-Roussel, 2023). Managers may perceive this new technology as a potential threat, leading them to take measures to fortify their authority by restricting digitally literate employees from accessing the informative potential of the technology. Even if employees are effectively prohibited from accessing the technology through legitimate internal channels, they may circumvent corporate barriers and utilize unauthorized external channels to ensure access to the technology (Alter, 2014). Top managers might impede, resist, or reject initiatives promoting transparency and inclusion in strategy-making (Hautz et al., 2017). Moreover, they are generally reluctant to relinquish control, such as by delegating decision-making rights (Hautz et al., 2019). Notably, Peng et al. (2020) discovered a positive relationship between transformational leadership and openness.

5.2 Digital tools for open strategies

Tacit and embedded knowledge in the organizational context should be considered in the frameworks of conceptual knowledge transfers. Obviously, transferring knowledge and novel ideas meets various barriers – not only specific human resistance to change and advancement in education, but it also combines difficulties in transferring different contexts. Moreover, transferring knowledge and ideas relies on the prime identification of generic reservoirs of the latter. Transfer of knowledge and ideas in organizations, in fact, can be labelled as a specific process of their diffusion among entities (people) in the bounded (limited) environment on the one hand, while on the other this process is prone to the inflow of knowledge and ideas from the outside of the organization. To a large extent, this process of knowledge and ideas diffusion is highly determined by trajectories of interactions among people within the organization. Henceforth, one of the managers' major tasks is to facilitate this diffusion to make it fit new contexts and be beneficial for the organization. Facilitating the diffusion of knowledge and ideas within the organization can derive internal competitive advantage over the local and global market, which at the same time allows preventing their external transfer to the competitors. Preventing the knowledge and ideas outflow seems crucial, even though it is kind of obvious that such transfers are more likely to happen within rather than between organizations. However, the process of embedding knowledge and ideas in people interaction can foster both their internal and external transfers.

The issue of knowledge and ideas transfers is subjected to firms' capabilities in this regard. Such capabilities are not granted, are not a given endowment, and hence organization may significantly differ, which affects their competing abilities. In this context, maximizing the positive effects, generating synergies and spillovers, and, as a consequence, knowledge and ideas transfer are fundamental. This element can also be regarded in a broader sense. As already argued, implementing an open strategies approach in companies constitutes an essential element of their growth and development, gaining in terms of competitive advantage and solid market position. In that sense, knowledge and ideas transferring and open strategizing relying on transparency and inclusiveness are inherently interrelated.

Following the claims raised in previous chapters, implementation of an open strategy requires, first of all, extensive transparency and inclusiveness at the organizational level (Whittington et al., 2011; Hautz et al., 2017). If we add the general necessity of agility, flexibility, and reflexives, there arises a picture of an organization, of a company, where the flow of knowledge and ideas is not only not bounded or restricted but is massively enhanced since the company's managers' intention is to benefit from greater openness and people's engagement. Digital technologies, in a broad sense, can effectively enhance inclusion and transparency not only in society and economy but also at meso and micro levels, hence in various types of organizations. However, although we see evidence (Cai et al., 2020; Li et al., 2020) supporting our claims that digital technologies change the companies' environment, both enhancing and enforcing profound changes in management strategies, it seems vital to consider that digital technologies offer a significant bundle of tools empowering open strategy implementation (Tavakoli et al., 2017).

On one hand, growing innovativeness drives broader adoption of ICT/IT tools in companies, while, on the other, ICT/IT tools dynamize the 'innovative culture' (Bendak et al., 2020; Hooi & Chan, 2023; Alshuhumi et al., 2024), upgrading and altering the firm's systems and tools already adopted. Innovative firms, once they head towards open strategy, adopt IT tools to recognize, collect, and diffuse knowledge and ideas, the IT tools – like for instance intranets, internal forums, and platforms – create awareness and engagement, provide support for higher-level managers in terms of information flows, and, finally, advocate for increasing innovativeness and growing competitive advantage. It is broadly agreed that different ICT/IT tools facilitate the intensive involvement of the company's stakeholders in the firm's functioning, generation of strategic content and knowledge, and intensification of ideas flows (Chesbrough & Appleyard, 2007; Wulf & Butel, 2016). Moreover, these ICT/IT tools are useful enough to engage stakeholders in providing their views and solution in the practice of strategy (Whittington et al., 2011; Whittington, 2014) and next implementation of this strategy. Digital technologies as network technologies (Fitzpatrick, 2000; Koper & Tattersall, 2004; Hidalgo et al., 2011) foster developing a network structure as a way to build global company. A network structure of a company, with a broad range of ICT/IT tools incorporated, encourages developing an atmosphere of openness and transparency, where employees and stakeholders are engaged and committed to designing and realization of a company's strategy. A network structure of a company, and IT-based platform networks (Haller et al., 2011; Bjørn-Andersen & Raymond, 2014) drive organizational internal dynamics, which is a key source of competitive advantage. In literature we find claims that that these IT-based platform networks implemented at the organizational level can even outmode the impact of a 'classical' network effects in its intensity. Such arguments have been raised in, for instance, Malhotra et al. (2017), referring to an online platform, and in Huang et al. (2013) and Baptista et al. (2017) to social media. Digital transformation, undoubtedly, is closely related to managerial work (Heavin & Power, 2018; De Bem Machado et al., 2022; Jafari-Sadeghi et al., 2023). Due to the digital tools (ICT/IT tools) adoption, companies can benefit through two major channels of impact. First, ICT/IT tools can make workflow and workforce management more effective and transparent; and second – the team management gains in its efficiency mainly due to timely information delivery, ability to meet instantly and connect instantly with other team members (through, for example, Ethernet-type solutions). These elements enforce companies to direct their efforts toward broader digital skills development among employees, which, in effect, drives intensive digitalization of various processes in an organization. Henceforth, a kind of synergy emerges. A good example of the latter may be the technology capability audit tool (CAT) (Rush et al., 2007 and 2014), designed to facilitate managers or other authorities to assess the level of organizational capabilities regarding digital skills and innovation readiness. In the open strategizing context, the CAT-like ICT/IT tools seems to be a perfect way to find the weakness of organizations that impede its transparency, inclusiveness, agility, and flexibility, ensuring greater openness of the company. Even though these few works emphasize the importance of these IT-based tools in enabling openness in a firm's strategy, so far the literature explaining more extensive and detailed adoption of digital technologies for these purposes is rather sporadic.

Still, a more extensive review of related literature signals the need for the adoption of ICT/IT tools in organizations implementing open strategies (Abbate et al., 2019). A brief summary suggests that, in the context of open strategy implementation, digital tools might be useful for the following purposes:

- Organizing the flow of ideas regarding possible triggers for changes and organizational and managerial adjustments
- Picking and identifying the signals on changing demands, consumers' needs and propensities, or any other changes in the outer environment
- Picking and structuring information about emerged new technological development and opportunities, new markets' potential marketing channels
- Examining and collecting information on employees' core competencies, regular auditing the latter, and identifying areas requiring upskilling and reskilling in order to stay competitive
- Identifying strategic priorities considering intersectional flows of ideas among organizational staff, which should include not only observed market trends but also clear and inclusive signalling of them to company members
- Permanent learning through developing of internal capabilities ensuring growth and development of the company

In a similar vein, in Kraft et al. (2022) we find claims on increasingly networked nature of people's relationships, which is one of the main consequence of the information and digital intensity of the environment. The leveraged networks – also these internal ones (as, for example, company's network platforms) – by bringing a massive stock of information, bring new values creation on board (Bauernhansl, 2017). Adopted in companies, 'digital tools are typically software applications and apps that exploit information abundance, computing power availability and connectivity to create new value' (Kraft et al., 2022, p. 472), and what is especially important in the context of open strategies, these new digital tools combine – vertically and horizontally – people and machines, enforcing the transparency and inclusiveness relying on the core of open strategies (Dröseln et al., 2017).

Goulart Heinzen & Lavarda (2021) emphasize that adoption of digital tools in organizations that implement open strategy allows controlling the closure paradox (Brogaard & Salerno, 2006; Ramachandran, 2016), for instance. Organization-wide adoption of digital tools (like, for instance, these developed by Jira Software allowing for reporting, designing agile boards and timelines) in companies implementing open strategy is useful to control and to avoid information overload and chaos, directions of information flows, and their usage can be adjusted to the desired level of openness at different organization levels. Moreover, specific ICT/IT tools allow for more structured and organized downward, upward, diagonal, and horizontal information flows to avoid white noise that may occur. In the extensive study of Baptista et al. (2017), we find evidence what of social media–type digital tools are adopted in organizations implementing open strategy. The cited research discusses a wide array of social media influencing over strategic activity in organizations. They show how digital tools like blogs, discussion forums, online communities, social network updates, or internal twitter, just to cite a few, impact the openness and transparency in an organization. From the collected surveys, they conclude that

> active use of social media to make the vision of senior management more transparent and gather support and feedback from employees. In some cases, this is used to define new strategic initiatives and support decision making. It also provides a view on employee sentiment for senior management.
>
> (Baptista et al., 2017, p. 324)

The same research also refers to different digital tools implemented in organizations, like post-meeting commenting forums, microblogging and instant messaging, polls and surveys, discussion groups, online portal for sharing feedback, and the seminal role of these tools in fostering within organization communication, enhancing inclusiveness and transparency. Needless to say that the within-organization platforms develop a kind of fast-track for communication channels, unveiling strong positive network externalities, and are perceived as strategic imperative, especially in the context of open strategy building. These digital tools allow creating unique spillover effects contributing to the organization's efficiency and efficacy (Wang et al., 2012; Cui et al., 2022).

5.3 Open strategy practices exemplars

Digital technologies are used in diversified contexts to support the strategizing process partially or fully. The vital and main question is not what should be used but to which extent the data would be revealed. Once the openness standpoint is specified, the decision on how to address it by supportive technology is made. Thus, when discussing the examples of practices exemplified by companies, we must consider the scope of openness that is applied, as it can be partial, full, or radical.

When we talk about partial openness, we may mention various forms that companies develop. At Zappos, to be in line with the declaration ('Build Open and Honest Relationships With Communication'), there is a dedicated department in the organization called Zappos Insights, which facilitates tours of the Zappos headquarters and live training events for anyone who is interested. Some of those activities are developed online (Zappos, 2024). Such practices allow the sharing of the corporate vision and observing the organizational climate, but also bring access to information by granting the possibility to exchange external ideas with employees. Moreover, access to information has been especially extended to the company's vendors, who can use a dedicated extranet tool to receive complete visibility into the business (Hsieh, 2013). Another illustration of partial openness is related to the supply chain context. The company Patagonia, as being focused on providing transparency throughout its supply chain and reducing any negative social and environmental impact, provided 'Footprint Chronicles' – publicly open videos related to particular products disclosing information about the suppliers and inviting any feedback from the customers on how to improve the supply process (Patagonia, 2024).

More advanced than partial is full openness. It may start with one of the most secretive areas – the salaries and payroll system. A transparent approach was introduced by Buffer company, which decided to fully reveal on their website the positions and the salaries assigned as well as the formula used to come up with their value (Buffer, 2024a). The drivers for this disclosure were twofold – enhancing the internal coherence but also sharing the experience and compensation strategy with other, less experienced market players, who can learn and benchmark the adopted practices. However, Buffer did not limit the openness to the payroll only, as they also decided to fully reveal the internal communication around COVID-19 they shared in 2020. In fact, the transparency strategy seems to be a well-designed and deliberate process as the company has presented a 'Timeline of transparency at Buffer' (Buffer, 2024b) where they share the formula for profit sharing and charitable contributions or even company budget and operating expenses. Buffers went even further as they disclosed a public Trello board with their up-to-date product roadmap, a description of the acquisition process, and even a public revenue dashboard with real-time revenue numbers. A full disclosure also involved the pricing breakdown with the graphics showing the exact division of paying every $10 and full information on what is calculated in a specific position. Transparency was the viewpoint adopted since the beginning as, at the end of 2011, the company announced that they had raised $450,000 and shared the names of the 19 investors and the way they were approached (Buffer, 2024b). All the data is publicly available on the website, and access is provided to the digital tools used in calculations or apps used by the company (i.e., Trello).

Finally, to illustrate radical openness, we may use the example of the company AIsthetic Apparel. That case illustrates a mixture of full openness with highly advanced digital technology as it is an AI-driven company selling T-shirts having AI-generated designs. The initial projections predict a €400,000 annual profit, which seems promising (Your story, 2023). The uniqueness and novelty of this business were based on giving full control to AI, which holds the CEO position. Since the beginning, the choice of the activity (product instead of service), market (fashion industry), name, and designs generated by Midjourney were instantly announced publicly, giving the full information to anyone interested. Moreover, a 10-point business plan with strategic decisions for launching an online store and developing the partnership with Printful was exposed, and full print screens with the prompts were available. AI was even able to suggest the investors and how to ensure the initial capital and calculate the price of the product. The sales value was shared with the community as the company achieved €10,000 in revenue within five days. All the plans were broadcast on LinkedIn, bringing significant attention with dozens of comments, tips, and suggestions from potential investors or customers as well as other interested parties (YourStory, 2024). As claimed on the company's website, it has been seen by more than ten million humans worldwide (AIsthetic Apparel, 2024). After the first month of operations, the company reported 8,538,906 impressions on LinkedIn and 120,000 EUR of capital raised from investors (LinkedIn, 2023a). Further steps, updates, and choices taken by the founders have been broadly discussed and reported, maintaining a high level of transparency and without any fear of imitation. As claimed by the founder, 'With generative AI creating a brand and putting an offer on the market to test consumer demand is close to zero' (LinkedIn, 2023b). Thus, the development of digital tools impacted the strategy communication and the strategizing process. Full transparency is no longer challenging as access to digital drivers is unrestricted and unlimited. The main concern is to provide the business value while offering the radical openness.

As we may see, the degree of openness is driven by various factors, mostly rooted in technological advancement and the tensions it brings. External stakeholders may impose transparency requirements, and strategizing standards may be set. But it may also be voluntary and bring the new competitive edge where the risk of imitation or replication is no longer valid. Due to digital technologies, the rules of the game have not only been changed but it even revolutionized and transformed the way of thinking about strategy.

References

Abbate, T., Codini, A. P., & Aquilani, B. (2019). Knowledge co-creation in open innovation digital platforms: Processes, tools and services. *Journal of Business & Industrial Marketing, 34*(7), 1434–1447.

Alshuhumi, S. R., Al-Hidabi, D. A., & Al-Refaei, A. A. A. (2024). Unveiling the behavioral nexus of innovative organizational culture: Identification and affective commitment of teachers in primary schools. *Journal of Human Behavior in the Social Environment, 34*(1), 130–152.

AIsthetic Apparel. (2024). Retrieved January 12, 2024, from https://aistheti-capparel.shop/

Alter, S. (2014). Theory of workarounds. *Communication Association Information Systems, 34*(55), 1041–1066.

Amrollahi, A., & Rowlands, B. (2017). Collaborative open strategic planning: A method and case study. *Information Technology People, 30*(4), 832–852.

Amrollahi, A., & Rowlands, B. (2018). OSPM: A design methodology for open strategic planning. *Information Management, 55*(6), 667–685.

Baptista, J., Wilson, A. D., Galliers, R. D., & Bynghall, S. (2017). Social media and the emergence of reflexiveness as a new capability for open strategy. *Long Range Planning, 50*(3), 322–336.

Bauernhansl, T. (2017). Die vierte industrielle Revolution–Der Weg in ein wertschaffendes Produktionsparadigma. *Handbuch Industrie 4.0 Bd. 4: Allgemeine Grundlagen*, 1–31.

Belmondo, C., & Sargis-Roussel, C. (2023). The political dynamics of opening participation in strategy: The role of strategy specialists' legitimacy and disposition to openness. *Organization Studies, 44*(4), 613–635.

Bendak, S., Shikhli, A. M., & Abdel-Razek, R. H. (2020). How changing organizational culture can enhance innovation: Development of the innovative culture enhancement framework. *Cogent Business & Management, 7*(1), 1712125.

Bjørn-Andersen, N., & Raymond, B. (2014). The impact of IT over five decades – Towards the ambient organization. *Applied Ergonomics, 45*(2), 188–197.

Brogaard, B., & Salerno, J. (2006). Knowability and a modal closure principle. *American Philosophical Quarterly, 43*(3), 261–270.

Brynjolfsson, E., & McAfee, A. (2014). *The second machine age: Work, progress, and prosperity in a time of brilliant technologies*. W. W. Norton & Company.

Buffer (2024a). Retrieved January 11, 2024, from https://buffer.com/salaries

Buffer (2024b). Retrieved January 11, 2024, from https://buffer.com/open

Cai, X., Zhu, B., Zhang, H., Li, L., & Xie, M. (2020). Can direct environmental regulation promote green technology innovation in heavily polluting industries? Evidence from Chinese listed companies. *Science of the Total Environment, 746*, 140810.

Chesbrough, H. W., & Appleyard, M. M. (2007). Open innovation and strategy. *California Management Review, 50*(1), 57–76.

Cui, T., Ye, J. H., & Tan, C. H. (2022). Information technology in open innovation: A resource orchestration perspective. *Information & Management, 59*(8), 103699.

Davison, R. M., & Ou, C. X. J. (2017). Digital work in a digitally challenged organization. *Information & Management, 54*(1), 129–137.

De Bem Machado, A., Secinaro, S., Calandra, D., & Lanzalonga, F. (2022). Knowledge management and digital transformation for Industry 4.0: A structured literature review. *Knowledge Management Research & Practice, 20*(2), 320–338.

Dröseln, J. K., Klünder, T., & Steven, M. (2017). Der industrie 4.0-Zyklus. Identifikaiton und Bewertung digitalisierungsinduzierter Risiken. *Industriemanagement*, *3*, 68–72.

Fitzpatrick, T. (2000). Critical cyberpolicy: Network technologies, massless citizens, virtual rights. *Critical Social Policy*, *20*(3), 375–407.

Goulart Heinzen, C., & Lavarda, R. A. B. (2021). Open strategizing activities & practices: The openness and closure paradox control by digital tools. In *Academy of management proceedings* (Vol. 2021, No. 1, p. 13981). Academy of Management.

Haller, J. B., Bullinger, A. C., & Möslein, K. M. (2011). Innovation contests: An IT-based tool for innovation management. *Business & Information Systems Engineering*, *3*, 103–106.

Hautz, J., Hutter, K., & Sutter, J. (2019). Practices of inclusion in open strategy. In D. Seidl, G. von Krogh & R. Whittington (Eds.), *Cambridge handbook of open strategy* (pp. 87–105). Cambridge University Press.

Hautz, J., Seidl, D., & Whittington, R. (2017). Open strategy: Dimensions, dilemmas, dynamics. *Long Range Planning*, *50*(3), 298–309.

Heavin, C., & Power, D. J. (2018). Challenges for digital transformation – towards a conceptual decision support guide for managers. *Journal of Decision Systems*, *27*(sup1), 38–45.

Hidalgo, R., Abbey, C., & Joós, G. (2011, July). Technical and economic assessment of active distribution network technologies. In *2011 IEEE power and energy society general meeting* (pp. 1–6). IEEE.

Hooi, L. W., & Chan, A. J. (2023). Does workplace digitalization matter in linking transformational leadership and innovative culture to employee engagement? *Journal of Organizational Change Management*, *36*(2), 197–216.

Hsieh, T. (2013). *Delivering happiness: A path to profits, passion, and purpose, grand central publishing*. Hachette Book.

Huang, P., Ceccagnoli, M., Forman, C., & Wu, D. J. (2013). Appropriability mechanisms and the platform partnership decision: Evidence from enterprise software. *Management Science*, *59*(1), 102–121.

Jafari-Sadeghi, V., Mahdiraji, H. A., Alam, G. M., & Mazzoleni, A. (2023). Entrepreneurs as strategic transformation managers: Exploring micro-foundations of digital transformation in small and medium internationalisers. *Journal of Business Research*, *154*, 113287.

Koper, R., & Tattersall, C. (2004). New directions for lifelong learning using network technologies. *British Journal of Educational Technology*, *35*(6), 689–700.

Kraft, C., Lindeque, J. P., & Peter, M. K. (2022). The digital transformation of swiss small and medium-sized enterprises: Insights from digital tool adoption. *Journal of Strategy and Management*, *15*(3), 468–494.

Li, Y., Dai, J., & Cui, L. (2020). The impact of digital technologies on economic and environmental performance in the context of industry 4.0: A moderated mediation model. *International Journal of Production Economics*, *229*, 107777.

LinkedIn (2023a). Retrieved January 12, 2024, from www.linkedin.com/posts/joao-ferrao-dos-santos_ecommerce-ai-gpt4-activity-7053396646742654976-Lt1X

LinkedIn (2023b). Retrieved January 12, 2024, from www.linkedin.com/company/aistheticapparel?trk=public_profile_topcard-current-company

Mack, D. Z., & Szulanski, G. (2017). Opening up: How centralization affects participation and inclusion in strategy making. *Long Range Planning*, *50*(3), 385–396.

Malhotra, N. K., Nunan, D., & Birks, D. F. (2017). *Marketing research: An applied approach*. Pearson.

Morton, J., Amrollahi, A., & Wilson, A. D. (2022). Digital strategizing: An assessing review, definition, and research agenda. *The Journal of Strategic Information Systems*, *31*(2), 101720.

Morton, J., Wilson, A. D., & Cooke, L. (2020). The digital work of strategists: Using open strategy for organizational transformation. *The Journal of Strategic Information Systems*, *29*(2), 101613.

Morton, J., Wilson, A. D., Galliers, R. D., & Marabelli, M. (2019). Open strategy and information technology. In D. Seidl, R. Whittington & G. von Krogh (Eds.), *Cambridge handbook of open strategy* (pp. 171–189). Cambridge University Press.

Orlikowski, W. J., & Scott, S. V. (2016). Digital work: A research agenda. In B. Czarniawska (Ed.), *A research agenda for management and organization studies* (pp. 88–96). Edward Elgar Publishing.

Patagonia. (2024). Retrieved January 11, 2024, from www.patagonia.com/where-we-do-business/

Peng, J., Li, M., Wang, Z., & Lin, Y. (2020). Transformational leadership and employees' reactions to organizational change: Evidence from a meta-analysis. *The Journal of Applied Behavioral Science*, *53*(3), 1–29.

Plotnikova, A., Pandza, K., & Sales-Cavalcante, H. (2021). How strategy professionals develop and sustain an online strategy community – the lessons from Ericsson. *Long Range Planning*, *54*(5).

Ramachandran, M. (2016). Knowledge-to-fact arguments (bootstrapping, closure, paradox and KK). *Analysis*, *76*(2), 142–149.

Richter, A., Heinrich, P., Stocker, A., & Schwabe, G. (2018). Digital work design: The interplay of human and computer in future work practices as an interdisciplinary (grand) challenge. *Business Information Systems Engineering*, *60*(3), 259–264.

Rush, H., Bessant, J., & Hobday, M. (2007). Assessing the technological capabilities of firms: Developing a policy tool. *R&d Management*, *37*(3), 221–236.

Rush, H., Bessant, J., Hobday, M., Hanrahan, E., & Medeiros, M. Z. (2014). The evolution and use of a policy and research tool: Assessing the technological capabilities of firms. *Technology Analysis & Strategic Management*, *26*(3), 353–365.

Sandeep, M. S., & Ravishankar, M. N. (2015). Social innovations in outsourcing: An empirical investigation of impact sourcing companies in India. *Journal Strategic Information Systems*, *24*(4), 270–288.

Schroll, A., & Mild, A. (2012). A critical review of empirical research on open innovation adoption. *Journal für Betriebswirtschaft*, *62*, 85–118.

Simeonova, B. (2018). Transactive memory systems and Web 2.0 in knowledge sharing: A conceptual model based on activity theory and critical realism. *Information Systems Journal*, *28*(4), 592–611.

Stieger, D., Matzler, K., Chatterjee, S., & Ladstaetter-Fussenegger, F. (2012). Democratizing strategy: How crowdsourcing can be used for strategy dialogues. *California Management Review, 54*, 44–68.

Tavakoli, A., Schlagwein, D., & Schoder, D. (2017). Open strategy: Literature review, re-analysis of cases and conceptualisation as a practice. *The Journal of Strategic Information Systems, 26*(3), 163–184.

Volberda, H. W., Khanagha, S., Baden-Fuller, C., Mihalache, O. R., & Birkinshaw, J. (2021). Strategizing in a digital world: Overcoming cognitive barriers, reconfiguring routines and introducing new organizational forms. *Long Range Planning, 54*(5), 102110.

Wang, N., Liang, H., Zhong, W., Xue, Y., & Xiao, J. (2012). Resource structuring or capability building? An empirical study of the business value of information technology. *Journal of Management Information Systems, 29*(2), 325–367.

Whittington, R. (2014). Information systems strategy and strategy-as-practice: A joint agenda. *The Journal of Strategic Information Systems, 23*(1), 87–91.

Whittington, R., Cailluet, L., & Yakis-Douglas, B. (2011). Opening strategy: Evolution of a precarious profession. *British Journal of Management, 22*(3), 531–544.

Wulf, A., & Butel, L. (2016). Knowledge sharing and innovative corporate strategies in collaborative relationships: The potential of open strategy in business ecosystems. In *Decision support systems VI-addressing sustainability and societal challenges: 2nd international conference, ICDSST 2016, Plymouth, UK, May 23–25, 2016, Proceedings 2* (pp. 165–181). Springer International Publishing.

Your Story. (2023). Retrieved January 12, 2024, from https://yourstory.com/2023/04/chatgpt-ai-ceo-profitable-startup-aisthetic-apparel

Zappos. (2024). Retrieved January 11, 2024, from www.zappos.com/about/how-we-work

6 Concluding remarks

A growing number of organizations apply openness as a principle of organizational functioning, guided by increasing participation and transparency of organizational processes (Hautz, 2017; Whittington et al., 2011). Today, openness is a principle that guides 'good' organizations, and transparency is a central element of this approach to strategy. Transparency is generally defined as the disclosure of information to the public and is a vital element of the open strategy approach. In this context, open strategy is also gaining importance in strategic processes. An open strategy is a set of practices that make actors' participation in the strategic process more transparent and/or inclusive (Hautz et al., 2017). Increasing stakeholder participation and transparency is intended to create space for greater creativity (Whittington et al., 2011; Stieger et al., 2012), joint building of meaning and shared awareness of problems among stakeholders (Seidl & Werle, 2018), more significant commitment to implementation strategy (Ketokivi & Castañer, 2004), and supports trust and legitimacy (Gegenhuber & Dobusch, 2017).

The discussion on the nature of open strategy also addresses the antecedents of the decision to open up a strategy (Adobor, 2020; Lavarda & Leite, 2022). This stream of research interest has been boosted recently as the increasing complexity of products and technologies, combined with rising costs, risks of innovation, and growing environmental uncertainty (Lavarda & Leite, 2022) are having an impact on the willingness of organizations to be more open (Durst & Ståhle, 2013; Baptista et al., 2017; Neeley & Leonardi, 2018; Whittington, 2019) and to develop cooperation agreements and partnerships (Crick & Crick, 2020). Indeed, the implementation of an effective organizational strategy '*nowadays is said to require open strategising practices*' (Doeleman et al., 2022, p. 54), which has been proven not only in the case of technologically advanced firms (e.g. those adopting platform-based business models – Cai & Canales, 2022) but also a wide range of SMEs (Bellucci et al., 2023), or even in the case of governmental organizations (Doeleman et al., 2022).

Open strategy is conceptualized in three approaches: practitioners, practices, and process (praxis), returning to the strategy-as-practice approach.

DOI: 10.4324/9781003424772-6

The practice perspective brings us closer to understanding individual practices and their elements (practice agent, artefacts, context, and emerging actions). This approach allows for a clear departure from the broad context of general social practices with attention to the components of practice (Levina & Arriaga, 2014; Gaskin et al., 2014; Nicolini, 2009). In this way, from the practice perspective, the process is visible in its relational setting. Viewing open strategy as a new practice rather than a new entity or process allows us to look at this holistic concept (Tavakoli et al., 2017).

In previous research, open strategy practitioners were the focal point of the process and interests. Differences between participants at different hierarchical levels were pointed out (Laari-Salmela et al., 2015), as well as the roles of external animators in an open strategy (e.g. Morton et al., 2016). Strategy practitioners may come from different levels of the organizational hierarchy, representing the highest levels, middle management levels, or outsiders (e.g. consultants) (Mirabeau & Maguire, 2014; Whittington, 2006). The latter are more closely identified with the highest levels for a specific period when performing the assigned activity. During the strategy process, practitioners use strategic decision-making practices developed in the organization (Whittington, 2006). However, external consultants can use other practices to which they have access, which provides additional value compared to those practices available only to managers.

The open strategy stream of research has recently intensified due to the growing importance of pressure on organizations to move towards greater strategic agility, combined with the ongoing tensions and challenges imposed by digital transformation and ICT development (Baptista et al., 2017; Neeley & Leonardi, 2018; Cai & Canales, 2022). The latter include, inter alia, automation of labour and digitally oriented strategy design (AlNuaimi et al., 2022), as well as data management (Morton et al., 2019). Digital technologies are changing the game's rules in many industry sectors regarding where and how to compete, what business model to choose, and the relative importance of creating versus capturing value. Digital technologies also enable changes in the internal structure and organization of companies' activities (Birkinshaw, 2018) and achieve the fluidity and routines required in digital environments (Rossi et al., 2020).

Openness is becoming an increasingly common formula of action treated as a new form of organizing (Puranam et al., 2014), and technology plays a key role both in who is included in processes and to what extent information is shared (Faraj et al., 2016; Kornberger et al., 2017). Digital context and IT are components and central parts of strategic practices that are widely implemented. An open strategy, therefore, provides a rich field for a better understanding of the relationship between IT and practitioners. There are many examples of organizations that experiment and implement various digital work tools used in strategizing practices, leading to the reconfiguration of work practices toward open strategizing. Analysis of these practices enriches our understanding of the benefits and limitations of the open strategizing process.

In considering openness and, consequently, open strategizing, one must recognize various conditions that can significantly facilitate or impede, even entirely, the implementation of openness in organizational processes, including strategic ones. Like any concept, openness requires process participants to possess specific skills, behaviours, and attitudes. The development of social media, in particular, blurs the boundaries between the real and virtual worlds. Furthermore, communication barriers disappear, and there is an increase in the courage to comment and express opinions in the hope or even the belief of remaining anonymous.

Therefore, looking from the perspective of individual entities potentially involved in open processes, one might argue that a certain level of maturity is expected, linked to awareness of individual influence on organizational processes. However, the elements associated with the development of online spaces make almost everyone feel the need to influence, even in the form of expressing opinions. This undoubtedly poses a significant challenge for contemporary managers who grapple daily with such expectations, although they may need more time to be ready for such solutions.

Managers' attitudes can determine organizational openness, especially strategic openness. Some managers perceive themselves as omnipotent, while others fear the loss of authority and position, at least formally, as strategy leaders. Although one might assume that the extent to which managers are willing to trust employees and outline the scope of autonomy, indicating the space for action, reflects more on the manager's authority than simply the position held.

In the end, contextual factors determine the possibilities and ultimately the extent of openness in organizational processes. However, one should not limit thinking to technology and access to digital tools. The specificity of processes, the nature of activities, and organizational culture are just some of the conditions that can either facilitate or hinder the creation of space for openness in processes.

Examples of practices that vary depending on the scope of openness that the company employs, as it could be partial, full, or radical, exemplify the scope of application and experimentation with the concept of openness. Regardless of the level of disclosure, all the practices were driven by digital technologies – either as enablers or factors that force the company to reveal strategic themes. Boosted transparency standards have become commonly accepted and transformed the way of building competitive advantage. Scarce resources become publicly available, and the risk of revealing the sensitive data has been commonly accepted. In exchange, companies receive the opportunity to gather the feedback, use the tacit external knowledge, and reshape the way of doing business. The pivotal questions arise not around if but how to use the digital context to balance the risk and reward of openness and to which extent the strategizing could or even should be further transformed. Using AI would play a vital role in addressing those concerns, and redefining the strategy practices would become a cognitive managerial dilemma.

References

Adobor, H. (2020). Open strategy: Role of organizational democracy. *Journal of Strategy and Management*, *13*, 310–331. https://doi.org/10.1108/JSMA-07-2019-0125

AlNuaimi, B. K., Kumar Singh, S., Ren, S., Budhwar, P., & Vorobyev, D. (2022). Mastering digital transformation: The nexus between leadership, agility, and digital strategy. *Journal of Business Research*, *145*, 148–2963. https://doi.org/10.1016/j.jbusres.2022.03.038

Baptista, J., Wilson, A. D., Galliers, R. D., & Bynghall, S. (2017). Social media and the emergence of reflexiveness as a new capability for open strategy. *Long Range Planning*, *50*, 322–336. https://doi.org/10.1016/J.LRP.2016.07.005

Bellucci, C. F., Lavarda, R. A. B., & Eliete Floriani, D. (2023). Open strategizing and accelerated internationalization process in different contexts. *Journal of Strategy and Management*, *16*, 189–210. https://doi.org/10.1108/JSMA-10-2021-0207/FULL/PDF

Birkinshaw, J. (2018). How is technological change affecting the nature of the corporation? *Journal of the British Academy*, *6*(s1), 185–214.

Cai, J., & Canales, J. I. (2022). Dual strategy process in open strategizing. *Long Range Planning*, *55*, 102177. https://doi.org/10.1016/J.LRP.2021.102177

Crick, J. M., & Crick, D. (2020). Coopetition and COVID-19: Collaborative business-to-business marketing strategies in a pandemic crisis. *Industrial Marketing Management*, *88*, 206–213. https://doi.org/10.1016/j.indmarman.2020.05.016

Doeleman, H. J., van Dun, D. H., & Wilderom, C. P. M. (2022). Leading open strategizing practices for effective strategy implementation. *Journal of Strategy and Management*, *15*, 54–75. https://doi.org/10.1108/JSMA-09-2020-0253

Durst, S., & Ståhle, P. (2013). Success factors of open innovation – a literature review. *International Journal of Business Research and Management*, *4*, 111–131.

Faraj, S., von Krogh, G., Monteiro, E., & Lakhani, K. R. (2016). Special section introduction: Online community as space for knowledge flows. *Information Systems Research*, *27*, 668–684.

Gaskin, J., Berente, N., Lyytinen, K., & Yoo, Y. (2014). Toward generalizable sociomaterial inquiry: A computational approach for zooming in and out of sociomaterial routines. *MIS Quarterly*, *38*(3), 849–A12.

Gegenhuber, T., & Dobusch, L. (2017). Making an impression through openness: How open strategy-making practices change in the evolution of new ventures. *Long Range Planning*, *50*, 337–354.

Hautz, J. (2017). Opening up the strategy process – a network perspective. *Management Decision, 55*, 1956–1983.

Ketokivi, M., & Castañer, X. (2004). Strategic planning as an integrative device. *Administrative Science Quarterly, 49*(3), 337–365.

Kornberger, M., Meyer, R. E., Brandtner, C., & Höllerer, M. A. (2017). When bureaucracy meets the crowd: Studying 'open government' in the Vienna city administration. *Organization Studies, 38*, 179–200.

Laari-Salmela, S., Kinnula, M., & Väyrynen, K. (2015). Participation in open strategy: Sharing performances and opening backstages in acts of strategy. In *Academy of Management Proceedings,* 1.

Lavarda, R. A. B., & Leite, F. K. (2022). Open strategizing and organizational resilience considering the environmental uncertainty. *Revista Ibero-Americana de Estratégia, 21*, e21447. https://doi.org/10.5585/RIAE. V21I2.21447

Levina, N., & Arriaga, M. (2014). Distinction and status production on user-generated content platforms: Using Bourdieu's theory of cultural production to understand social dynamics in online fields. *Information Systems Research, 25*(3), 468–488.

Mirabeau, L., & Maguire, S. (2014). From autonomous strategic behaviour to emergent strategy. *Strategic Management Journal, 35*, 1202–1229.

Morton, J., Wilson, A., & Cooke, L. (2015). Collaboration and knowledge sharing in open strategy initiatives. In *iFutures 2015. Sheffield iSchool Conferences.* 10.13140/RG.2.1.2433.9042/2

Morton, Josh, Alexander D. Wilson, and Louise Cooke. 2019. "Open Strategy Initiatives: Open, It-enabled Episodes of Strategic Practice". *figshare.* https://hdl.handle.net/2134/22071.

Morton, J., Wilson, A., Galliers, R. D., & Marabelli, M. (2019). Open strategy and information technology. In G. Seidl, D. Whittington & R. von Krogh (Eds.), *Cambridge handbook of open strategy* (pp. 169–185). Cambridge University Press. https://doi.org/10.1017/9781108347921.011

Neeley, T. B., & Leonardi, P. M. (2018). Enacting knowledge strategy through social media: Passable trust and the paradox of nonwork interactions. *Strategic Management Journal, 39*, 922–946. https://doi.org/10.1002/ SMJ.2739/EPDF

Nicolini, D. (2009). Zooming in and out: Studying practices by switching theoretical lenses and trailing connections. *Organization Studies, 30*(12), 1391–1418.

Puranam, P., Alexy, O., & Reitzig, M. (2014). What's "new" about new forms of organizing? *Academy of Management Review, 39*, 162–180.

Rossi, M., Nandhakumar, J., & Mattila, M. (2020). Balancing fluid and cemented routines in a digital workplace. *The Journal of Strategic Information Systems, 29*(2), 101616

Seidl, D., & Werle, F. (2018). Inter-organizational sensemaking in the face of strategic meta-problems: Requisite variety and dynamics of participation. *Strategic Management Journal, 39*, 830–858.

Stieger, D., Matzler, K., Chatterjee, S., & Ladstaetter-Fussenegger, F. (2012). Democratizing strategy: How crowdsourcing can be used for strategy dialogues. *California Management Review, 54*, 44–68.

Tavakoli, A., Schlagwein, D., & Schoder, D. (2017). Open strategy: Literature review, re-analysis of cases and conceptualisation as a practice. *The Journal of Strategic Information Systems, 26*(3), 163–184.

Whittington, R. (2006). Completing the practice turn in strategy research. *Organization Studies, 27,* 613–634.

Whittington, R. (2019). *Opening strategy: Professional strategists and practice change, 1960 to today.* Oxford University Press.

Whittington, R., Cailluet, L., & Yakis-Douglas, B. (2011). Opening strategy: Evolution of a precarious profession. *British Journal of Management, 22,* 531–544.

Index